# Manston's
# Flea Markets

Antique Shows, and Auctions

# of FRANCE

# Manston's
# Flea Markets

## Antique Shows, and Auctions

# of FRANCE

Including
where to find markets,
how to ship items, clear customs, and much more

by
Peter B. Manston

A Travel Key Guide
Published by Travel Keys
Sacramento, California U.S.A.

Published by Travel Keys
in association with Prima Publishing
and distributed by St. Martin's Press

Travel Keys
P. O. Box 160691
Sacramento, California 95816 U.S.A.
Telephone (916) 452-5200

Prima Publishing
P.O. Box 1260
Rocklin, California 95677
Telephone (916) 624-5718

St. Martin's Press
175 Fifth Ave.
New York, New York 10010
(212) 674-5151

Designed by Peter B. Manston
Editing and cover photo by Robert C. Bynum
Illustrations by Claudia R. Graham
Type galleys by The Electric Page
Printed and bound by Arcata Graphics
Manufactured in the United States of America
First Printing January 1987

**Library of Congress Cataloguing in
Publication Data**
Manston, Peter B., 1951-
  Manston's flea markets, antique shows, and auctions of France.
  "A Travel Key Guide." Includes index.
   1. Flea markets—France. 2. Antiques—France—Exhibitions. 3. Auctions—France.    I. Title. II. Title: Flea markets, antique shows, and auctions of France. III. Title: Antique Shows.
HF5482.M313   1987        381'.1        86-30909
ISBN 0-931367-06-9

# Contents

## Acknowledgements

Many people helped provide information and support during the time while this book was written. Most of them provided help, but it isn't possible to thank them all. A few I'd like to specially thank include: Robert C. Bynum, who aided in field research and provided excellent editorial comments and moral support, Paula R. Mazuski for help in clarifying the objective of this book, and Agnes A. Manston (my mother). In addition, we appreciate the help of Will Renner, Bernadette Meauze, Frank Patch, and Sam Toll.

## Disclaimer of Responsibility

# Introduction

You will find flea markets, antique fairs, and auction houses just about everywhere in France—they burst forth in some of the most unlikely places like crocuses blooming through spring snow. Like crocuses, they are tough in spite of their apparent fragility—many have been held at the same location for decades and some for centuries.

At flea markets, antique hand-blown crystal decanters sit next to dusty bronze statues, paintings of indefinite age, all supported by old furniture, rickety tables, permanent stands, or, sometimes, only by the timeworn cobblestones of the street. The babble and hubbub of hundreds of voices makes the scene exciting, full of local color. You can find anything and everything at these flea markets—sinks, scrap metal, old clothes, and cabbages. Though a lot is just plain junk, there are a few lurking treasures.

At hundreds of antique shows and fairs, thousands of dealers display long rows of exquisitely-nurtured antiques of all types and ages: Louis XV furniture, gold 19th-century mantel clocks, and fine, massive silver.

Every region of France has public auctions: the types of items sold under the auctioneer's hammer is unlimited in its variety, from paintings, tapestries, and carpets to old farm implements and country furniture.

In this book, you'll find information vital to the antique dealer and collector:
- when and where to find flea markets, auctions, and shows
- basic flea market French
- how to ship your purchases home safely
- export requirements for taking fine arts and antiques and fine arts out of France
- U.S. and Canadian Customs requirements for getting items home
- and much, much more.

To make this book easy to use, a complete index will help you find what you need fast.

This book is dedicated to you, the ever-hopeful collector of exciting experiences and warm memories.

# Can You Still Make Finds?

All of us have heard about long-lost masterpieces found in a junk shop or bought for a few dollars at a flea market. We would all like to make a "great find"—a long lost Watteau, perhaps, or an original Toulouse-Lautrec poster, a piece of original Louis XV furniture, or a solid silver chocolate pot.

These items do exist, and can occasionally be found, usually accompanied by great publicity and newspaper headlines. Finds of this type are rare.

But minor finds can more readily be made—the antique solid silver serving spoon for much less than the cost of silver plate, the finely-detailed century-old newel post wood carving, a minor artist's 17th- or 18th-century painting.

The more you know about a given period or class of objects, the likelier you are to recognize and make a true find. This merely reinforces the fact that specialized knowledge has potentially great value.

Remember, you're searching for the proverbial needle in a haystack; there are thousands of French dealers and collectors in competition for the same things you are. You, however, can have the advantage of broader exposure, and you know about a radically different antique market unknown to most of the French: the United States and Canadian market, where there is a smaller selection of items that sell for significantly higher prices.

Since many European dealers only know about specialties of their own locality or country, you can take the broader view, surveying the products of the entire continent. Often, your best finds will be products or artwork far from their home, and therefore, whose true value is unappreciated or unknown locally.

# Why Search for Antiques in France?

The great artistry of French craftsmen has been renowned for centuries, even before the 17th century golden age of Louis XIV, the "Sun King," and its dedication to absolute luxury. You find proof in soaring Gothic cathedrals, exquisite detail of Gobelins tapestries, and fine woodwork ranging from inlaid marquetry secretaires to massive country armoires.

France's rich heritage of careful and almost faultless craftsmanship remains active. Today, the best French work for the luxury market is famous for its style and quality.

Only Germany and Britain have as many different markets as France. But no country exceeds France in the variety and quality of items to be found. Though in the years just after World War II antiques and collectables could be found for a trifle, most French today are aware of the value of the things they want to sell. In many cases, though, French prices are far lower than those found in the United States or Canada, and often less than Germany or Switzerland for equivalent work. Of course, the relative strength of dollars, marks, and Belgian and Swiss francs against the French franc could change this. This doesn't mean that things are dirt cheap—only less expensive. What will not change is that France has a much greater wealth of antiques and collectables than you'll find at home.

The world's prototype flea market is the Paris' Marché aux Puces at the Porte de Saint-Ouen and the Porte de Clignancourt. There is probably no larger market or larger single concentration of antiques, collectables, and junk in the world. Situated just outside the site of ancient but long demolished city walls, the market arose when the city of Paris forbade throwing trash into the streets. Instead, it had to be thrown into containers. Then the trash was all carted to this tumbledown habitat of garbage haulers and scavengers. The trash was picked over, and anything salvageable was offered for sale: used clothes, broken furniture, discarded silver, and broken crystal.

Though still grimy and weatherbeaten, this area no longer resembles a garbage dump. Neither do most of the flea markets elsewhere in Paris and the rest of France.

Most French markets and fairs are regional in scope: while Paris draws on the rich heritage of all of France, traditionally rich regions (such as Burgundy and Normandy), and cities (such as Lyon and Bordeaux) have much of local origin to offer. The untouristed, economically declining industrial area around Lille, almost on the Belgian border, also has much to offer the collector and dealer.

Regions in the relatively poor mountain ranges of central France have far less to offer, though finds of folk art (both new and old) can be made by the careful buyer. It's just that there's much less to choose from, though the scenery and rustic charm of these regions alone can justify a visit.

French markets in all but the largest cities are often mixed: antiques and junk form but a small part of the larger market, full of everyday products such as new clothes, kitchen gadgets, cheap plastic items, and, above all, food. While often the antique and junk sellers congregate in a particular part of the market or occupy only one street or small square, sometimes the various kinds of sellers are happily intermingled: an old peasant may sell carrots, potatoes, and delicate heads of Boston-type lettuce next to a whole family selling kitchen items and small, plastic, car-size carpet sweepers, while a young, intense man sells old bottles, tarnished silver plate, and a beautiful late 19th-century cut glass crystal wine carafe.

Search for antiques in France because the variety is endless, the quality of the items is high, and because it's challenging and fun.

# Learning to Know What You See

In France, you'll find antiques, collectables, and assorted items by the thousands. You're limited only by your money, your patience, and your transportation. Good luck and intuition may help you discover an item of real artistic quality, but for the real finds, you must know what you're looking at.

You'll be well repaid later by the effort spent now, when you will know enough to tell a good piece from a poor or fake one while on your own at a boisterous flea market, auction, or antique show. You'll be faced with hundreds and thousands of items, but only a few will interest you, and even fewer will be a very good value for the serious collector.

At well-known dealers and dealers' marts, such as the Louvre des Antiquaires in Paris or Brocante Stalingrad in Lyon, you will often be able to obtain certificates of authenticity and provenance papers, in which the vendor states that you're really buying an antique. Naturally such guarantees and paperwork have their (high) price.

At flea markets and junk shops, however, the motto is "let the buyer beware." The market in fakes sold to the unwary is large, and buyers' cupidity and ignorance are prime sales tools for these sellers.

The time to start learning is right now. Read everything you can—style guides, price guides, antique-trade and fine arts magazines, museum catalogues, and applied arts and fine arts history. Catalogues from Christie's and Sotheby's auctions are treasure-troves of knowledge, with illustrations of sale items, descriptions of the creators, the items, and characteristics of the styles, and estimated sales prices. These catalogues are sometimes available at libraries and museums and, of course, are sold through the auction houses.

Study the text and illustrations carefully—what you remember will make it much easier to sort through the thousands of worthless pieces for the few excellent items later.

Your local library is an excellent place to begin. Look through the "Books In Print" to supplement your search of library shelves—many small and medium-sized libraries can often obtain books through an "interlibrary loan" system. For details and to make a request, see the reference librarian.

College and university libraries have more complete and specialized collections. Usually the public is admitted to "open-stack" libraries and can read the books in the library at no charge. Often you can become a "friend of the library" at modest cost to obtain borrowing privileges.

Museums are another place to learn. In major museums you will be able to see actual examples of authentic, good-quality works. Study the lines, the artistic qualities, and materials carefully. When you have a bit of knowledge but want more, seek out the curators in the museum. If you're particularly interested, curators and staff members can and often will make materials and items available to you. Remember that many museums have much of their collection in storage—there's rarely enough space to display everything. Show at least rudimentary knowledge and scholarly intent to obtain the maximum amount of help and access. Sometimes museums also have excellent art libraries.

Antique dealers in your area represent a valuable source of knowledge. Usually they have specialties, though the most knowledgeable, specialized and expensive dealers are clustered in cities such as New York, Boston, Chicago, San Francisco, Los Angeles, and Toronto. Experts love to share their knowledge with an appreciative audience.

Let your sense of beauty and value for money guide you: learn to trust your instincts, based on a foundation of knowledge.

# Origins of the Flea Market

Centuries ago, as the people living in the Middle Ages prospered, European cities began to grow, stimulated by trade in the cloth, foods, and other products of other parts of Europe, and the luxuries of the east.

Great markets and fairs were held in the centers that developed at trade route crossroads, such as Bruges, Ghent, Frankfurt, Lyon, Paris, and Milan. From these, the idea of regular scheduled markets specializing in certain products arose. In a world of slow and uncertain transport (ships pushed by sails, loaded carts drawn by animals, or packs carried by human porters), fairs offered an efficient way to exchange goods, meet new people, and hear news of and see exotic products from far-off places. Today's exquisite annual or biennial antique fairs and weekend flea markets are direct descendents of these fairs.

Though trade increased, material goods were still scarce, and used longer than they are today. Municipal garbage collection service did not exist: instead, some items were sold to roving junk dealers. The rest was thrown in the street, where rag pickers and junk men took leftover and discarded goods, sorted through them at home, and salvaged whatever had any value for reuse or resale. The items were sold in the neighborhoods where the rag pickers lived. One of the largest and most famous rag pickers' neighborhoods was just outside the Paris city walls at the Porte de Saint-Ouen. This area, especially since World War II, has become what is probably the largest flea market in Europe, and possibly in the world.

In large cities such as Calcutta and Cairo, Manila and Mexico City, trash is still disposed of in a similar way.

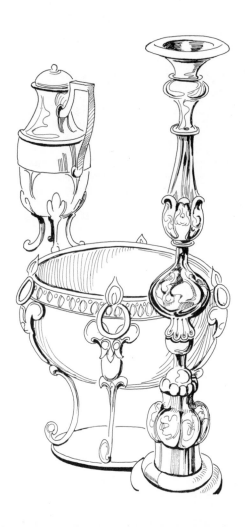

# Types of Markets

France's hundreds of markets divide into several types, which are roughly similar to the types of markets in other countries.

You should always try to get a receipt for every purchase. It is needed for Customs when you return home. However, some sellers, especially at flea markets, may be unwilling to give you a written receipt, or will give you an inadequate or illegible receipt. If you can't get an adequate receipt, keep a record of the date, location, description of the item, and price you paid.

### Marché aux puces (flea market)

The flea market, especially common in large cities, offers used items and often antiques. Sometimes these are held indoors in semi-permanent or permanent booths, but most often they are held outside or in a public market hall. Dealers may sell new items and reproductions as well as junk and antiques, so check potential purchases carefully.

### Marché à la brocante (junk market)

The category of "brocante" includes and centers on old, decrepit items in need of restoration. A vendor of "brocante" at the market implies that the odd miscellany of items all came from his great grandmother's attic in their ancestral farmhouse in the country. A shop selling "brocante" implies dim rooms filled with dusty furniture and other items untouched for decades.

### Salon des antiquaires
(antique dealers' salon) sometimes called "Foire des antiquités" (antiques fair)

Vendors at this type of market must be antique dealers, who sell items that come from their shops. Some dealers exclusively work the fairs and shows and do not have shops or warehouses open to the public. However, you can often obtain access to their warehouses by appointment.

Items at fairs are often guaranteed to be antiques; many fairs and salons explicitly ban all reproductions, and have legally certified experts to insure authenticity. Antique fairs (and shops) imply that these wonderful items have been exquisitely cared for, and are equally quite suitable for an elegant chateau, city penthouse, or restored and luxurious manor house.

# Auctions

**Scope of Auctions**

A large proportion of used items and antiques
pass through public sales hall auctions. Many
bidders are antique dealers, some are collectors, few are foreigners. With a limited number
of bidders, most of whom know the territory,
auctions often offer much better bargains than
shops or antique shows and salons, and often
offer a better quality of merchandise than
street fairs and flea markets.

**Where auctions are held**

*Paris*

Most important art and antique auctions take
place in Paris, at the Hôtel Drouot, the location
not far from the Opéra and Grands
Boulevards, widely acknowledged as the center
of the French antique trade.

    Here, nestled among hundreds of dealers, you
find sales halls, auctioneers' offices, shippers and
freight forwarders, consolidators, and experts
to study and warrant that the item is as claimed,
and who can deal with the French customs and
export control agents.

*The Provinces*

Most French cities and some provincial towns have public auction halls (Salles des Ventes) where auctions are held on a regular basis. When a town has a public auction hall, the usual sale days, addresses, and phone numbers of the hall are included in the detailed town listings.

## Finding Auctions and Auction Dates

Most regular auction sales are listed here in the town-by-town section. They can be relied upon, since many have been continuously in business for decades.

Inspection of merchandise and buyer registration is held the day before and the morning of the sale. Often there is no opportunity to inspect items when the sale actually begins, usually at 2 p.m. in the north of France and at 2:30 p.m. in the south.

Special auctions, whether held in Paris or in the provinces, are almost without exception listed in the weekly antique trade newspaper, La Gazette de l'Hôtel Drouot.

This publication can be obtained at the Hôtel Drouot, and at some newstands, and through the publisher:

La Gazette de l'Hôtel Drouot
99 rue de Richelieu
75002 Paris
Telephone 42.61.81.78.

Specialized antiques and arts magazines will often have listings announcing special auctions. Coverage in daily and weekly general circulation newspapers will have some information about auctions and antique shows, but they will usually be on a space-available basis and are sometimes incomplete.

## How to Participate

Depending on the auctioneer and the auction house, bidding can be as easy as raising your hand or catching the auctioneer's eye with a nod of your head. In other auctions, you may pre-register at the reception desk. In any case, ask at the reception desk before the auction begins.

You will at least need to understand French numbers, to ensure that you know how much you bid. In addition, at least a rudimentary knowledge of French will help. Also, knowledge of the items will be useful; although the auctioneer may describe the items your own knowledge is more reliable.

Payment is in cash, or a check drawn in French Francs on a French bank with acceptable identification (usually a carte d'identité for French residents, carte de séjour for foreign residents of France, or a passport for non-resident foreigners).

## Right to a Receipt

You have the right to receive a written receipt for every item you buy at auction. It will be the correct amount, since the auctioneer is legally bound by it.

## Taxes and Commissions

You will be responsible for paying the 6% tax on transfers of antiques, and 17.29% a value-added tax ("Taxe sur la Valeur Ajoutée", usually written as TVA) on the sales commission. You may also have to pay part of the sales commission, although the seller will pay most of this.

## Regulation of Auctioneers and Auctions

French auctions of all types are closely regulated by the government and trade groups. While auctions may be sponsored by various organizations, only a licensed individual auctioneer ("commissaire- priseur") may actually conduct an auction. Auctioneers are personally responsible (and legally liable) for all matters relating to the auctions they conduct.

The trade group, which provides professional standards and from whom information can be obtained and complaints made is:

Compagnie Nationale des Commissaires-
  Priseurs
13 rue de la Grange-Bâtelière
75009 Paris
Telephone 47.70.89.33.

# Who are the Sellers?

You always hope to find friendly, helpful vendors who don't know the value of what they're selling, and therefore will sell it to you for a song. While such sellers do exist, they are only slightly more common than hens' teeth.

Most sellers at flea markets and antique fairs are full-time dealers, who may close their regular shops or leave an assistant to mind the main store. Often, at permanent stands at major full-time flea markets such as Saint-Ouen in Paris, or along Boulevard Risso in Nice, it is the seller's only shop. Depending on the nature of the market, they either take their best or worst items to dispose of—whatever they think will sell.

Dealers' knowledge of their chosen field may vary widely. Many use reference books and price guides to help them keep track of their pricing. The day of the untutored and ignorant seller of antiques has passed almost completely.

Some vendors are junk dealers pure and simple, who drive around in trucks reading (translated) "I buy everything." They clean out basements and attics, old barns, warehouses, and garages. Some even go on early morning safaris looking for salvageable items in the trash! Regardless an item's origin, they may ask the amount listed in the price guides.

Part-time vendors are usually found in strength only at the weekend flea markets where permanent stands aren't available. During the week, they are members of other trades and professions. While many do not have the choicest items, they may be more willing to negotiate and they are often more willing to share experiences. Many of their items may only be of garage-sale or rummage-sale quality.

Many dealers have no fixed place of business, except their vans and trucks, and maybe a dusty barn at their home in the country. They serve as "pickers"—that is, picking up the best around the country, and serving as the city dealers' source of supply. If you can find them before the market opens, they can also serve you as a cheaper source of supply as well. These traveling dealers have the time and patience to seek out house sales, country auctions, and fund-raising sales of charity groups. They often cultivate a grapevine to lead to tips and sources of supply. Because they have no fixed place of business, they often thrive on large turnover and take low markups.

# Bargaining

Prices at flea markets and antique fairs are rarely fixed—you can usually obtain reductions of 10 to 50 per cent of the first asking price if you try. Knowing the economics of the market helps.

As a rule of thumb, most dealers try to double the prices of everything they sell. They feel entitled to this for their time, trouble, skill, and luck.

First prices asked almost always include a "fudge factor," since most sellers (and most buyers) expect to haggle and reduce the initial price. In fact, if you fail to bargain, some vendors may be puzzled and deprived of the conversational ritual to set the final price. The conversations as well as the money constitute much of the income many part time vendors expect and enjoy.

Here are a number of tactics to try to bring the price down:

1. The seller will always make a profit: his or her initial cost is also the base price. Some sellers keep markups low to increase turnover: this will make initial prices seem more reasonable, but there maybe less price flexibility.

If the dealer just obtained the item, the price may be reduced to provide a quick profit to raise cash. The dealer may know of another more desirable object he or she may need some added money to buy. On the other hand, if the item has been a long-time dust collector, and you're the first person even casually interested, the price may be less. If there's been a lot of inflation in the country, the seller may be thinking only of the original price paid.

2. The price is usually on an "as is—where is" basis. If there's an imperfection, use it as a way to try to reduce the price.

3. Bargain even if you know an item is an incredibly good buy. You can still always pay the initial asking price later. Failure to bargain may make the vendor believe that either you're foolish or that the item is very valuable (and it may be withdrawn from sale.)

4. Treat sellers as **people** first—this will solve many of your price problems. Politeness, courtesy, and consideration will make a difference.

5. Have at least a basic knowledge of the French language. The ability to communicate is invaluable at the market.

6. When you first see an item you want, set a price on it in your mind even before you pick it up to examine it. Don't pay more if you can help it. The "get it now" mentality used by auctioneers and high-pressure salespeople can lead you to spend far more than you planned. Conversely, there are sometimes a few items you must have, or you'll regret it forever.

7. If you find an item you know is unique, don't wait and plan to come back later. You probably won't, or it will be sold when you do come back. You may never see a similar item again, and be reminded of it every time you see the empty space on your mantel at home.

8. Don't make a beeline for the only item you want. Showing too much interest right off may lead to a higher final price. Better to pick up five or six items of lesser interest, and look at them as well as the items you want.

One maneuver that sometimes works well is to ask the price of a group of unrelated items, then ask the price of smaller groups, single items, and eventually ask the price of the item you really want.

Often, using this approach, the price of the item you want is less than its proportional share of the whole group—and a bargain besides.

## Two Afterthoughts

1. Some dealers are contrary and won't reduce the price at all. It may be only with a particular item, only with foreigners, or the color of your eyes. This is rare: firm prices are almost unknown at flea markets, and uncommon in fixed antique markets, even in the very exquisite and expensive Louvre des Antiquaires in Paris.

2. Have enough cash to buy what you want. At flea markets, all payments are expected to be cash—in the local currency. No checks, no credit cards, no foreign money such as dollars.

# What Season To Go?

### Flea Markets

Flea markets are held year-round in France, just as in the rest of the world. When you go is best determined by other needs, since each season has its special charm. The types of items will not change very much, except that new clothes and fresh vegetables (in those markets that have them) will follow the seasons.

Winter offers fewer markets, somewhat fewer sellers and prospective buyers, and certainly fewer tourists. (Bear in mind, however, that even in winter, you're clearly recognizable as a foreigner, often before you begin speaking.) With fewer buyers, pressure to reduce prices in serious bargaining may be stronger.

Spring is generally more rewarding than winter; not only are people coming out from the cold, but the seasonal flea markets begin to open. Spring cleaning may not be the best known tradition in much of Europe, but longer, warmer, sunnier days bring out more buyers and more sellers as well. Markets open in the morning as the days get longer.

Summer is the high season for the flea market trade. Tourists swarm across the continent; while there are several million from the U.S. and Canada, Europeans themselves outnumber everyone else many times over. Not only do most French workers usually get four or five weeks of paid vacation, they all try to take their vacations during the month of August.

During the summer season, bargaining may not always bring the lower prices often possible at other times of the year. On the other hand, summer is when many of the smaller, once-a-year countryside fairs and markets take place.

Fall is in many ways the most rewarding season to search the flea markets. The climate is still relatively mild, the seasonal flea markets are still operating (usually at least until the beginning of November), and most of the tourists have returned home.

## Auctions and Fairs

Auctions and antique fairs are held year-round. However, the best shows, sales and fairs usually take place in the fall, and to a slightly lesser degree in the Spring. Fairs in winter tend to be times when dealers stock up for the next spring and fall.

# Language

Don't know a word of French? Don't let that prevent you from going to flea markets and auctions in France! A surprising number of people speak at least a little English, the international language of commerce. It is required in many high schools and universities. Your best chance of finding someone speaking English is with a person of high school or college age.

Though knowledge of French gives you a real edge in bargaining, is isn't strictly required for successful flea marketing or purchases at shows. A slightly larger knowledge of French (especially numbers) is necessary at auctions.

You should, however, make an effort to learn at least a few words of French, such as the most important words "please," "thank you," and numbers.

By making the effort to communicate in the seller's native language, you'll engage the seller's sympathy, since they know you've made an effort.

The more you can speak, the more you can ask questions about any particular object, point out its defects, more forcefully haggle over the price, lead the conversation on interesting and price-softening digressions.

If you're a good listener, you'll learn about the item (or at least the range of the seller's knowledge), possibly its history and origin, how (but not usually where) it was found, and other interesting things. As you listen, you'll also get a conversational language course.

The next pages have the basic phrases needed to successfully buy at flea markets, shows, and auctions.

**Language Key**

| | |
|---|---|
| Good morning. . afternoon. | Bon jour. . . jour. |
| Please | S'il vous plaît |
| Thank you. | Merci. |
| Where is the flea market? | Où est le marché aux puces? |
| . . . junk market? | . . . le marché de la brocante? |
| . . . antique fair? | . . . foire d'antiquités? |
| . . . crafts market? | . . . le marché artisanal? |
| Over there. | Là bas. |
| Straight ahead. | Tout droit. |
| Right. Left. | A droit. A gauche. |
| Around the corner | Au coin de la rue. |
| Can you show me on the map? | Pouvez-vous me montrer sur la carte? |
| At the market | Au marché |
| How much (does this cost)? | Combien (est-ce)? |
| That is too much! | C'est trop cher! |
| What is it? | Qu'est-ce c'est? |
| How old is it? | Quel âge cela a-t-il? |
| How is it used? | Comment est-ce utilisé? |
| Does it work? | Est-ce que ça marche? |
| It's broken. Look here! | C'est cassé. Regardez ici! |
| What is it made out of? | De quoi est-ce fait? |
| Will you reduce the price? | Pouvez vous réduire le prix? |

| | |
|---|---|
| What is your lowest price? | Qual est le plus bas prix? |
| Can you take _____ francs? | Acceptez-vous _____ francs? |
| I don't have enough money. | Je n'ai pas assez argent. |
| Can I pay with dollars? | Est-ce que je peux payer avec des dollars? |
| I would like a receipt . . . | Je voudrais une facture . . |
| . . . for our Customs. | . . . pour la douane. |
| Where are the toilets? | Où sont les toilettes? |

0 zéro
1 un
2 deux
3 trois
4 quatre
5 cinq
6 six
7 sept
8 huit
9 neuf
10 dix
11 onze
12 douze
13 treize
14 quatorze
15 quinze
20 vingt
30 trente
40 quarante
50 cinquante
60 soixante
70 soixante-dix
80 quatre-vingt
90 quatre-vingt-dix
100 cent
200 deux cents
1,000 mille
2,000 deux mille
5,000 deux mille

| | |
|---|---|
| Thank you. | Merci. |
| Good by. | Au revoir. |

# Market Times and Places

Most flea markets start very early in the morning. To get a chance at the best of the newly arriving items, you need to arrive at the market as early as the local dealers and collectors. You also need convenient transportation for the specific markets and fairs you want to attend. Transport to weekday central city fairs or auctions calls for a very different transit strategy than a roving tour of country and suburban fairs and markets.

At flea markets in North America, a crowd gathers when a seller pulls into a space like bees gather around fragrant red flowers. In France, browsers also crowd around as the merchandise is unpacked. The first person to hold a treasure gets the first chance to examine and buy it. Even at the few markets (such as Paris' Clignancourt—Porte de Saint-Ouen) where some of the established booths and indoor shops don't open until 9 or 10 in the morning, sidewalk vendors arrive at dawn—and often leave by the time the indoor stores open and the large crowds arrive. Many times, you'll get better bargains from these early-bird sellers than from dealers in the shops and stalls.

### Food, Drink, and Toilets at the Flea Market

*Food at the Fair*

Most flea markets have food and drink at concession stands. Such convenience food, not noted for quality or good value, ranges from cans of soda pop to small pizzas, sandwiches, hamburgers, fried potatoes, as well as a wonderful array of large, domed loaves of country bread, homemade salami, and wines and cider sold by the producer.

Snack food sold at flea markets is usually as safe as any food elsewhere in France. Use the same precautions you would use anywhere.

If the market is part of a general market with fruit and vegetable vendors as well as antiques and junk, you may find better variety and more quality for your money.

*Toilets*

There are toilets at most flea markets or in the neighborhood. They may be primitive, smelly, and ill-maintained. There may not be any toilet paper. Some of the worst ones have attendants to collect money. If no toilets are visible, ask a seller—because they are familiar with the market.

Often facilities for women are unequal to the demand—plan to wait.

In a few major weekend flea markets in permanent, open-air locations, public toilets may be totally absent. In this case, there may be nearby bars or restaurants where you can find relief. You needn't be a patron—unless you see a sign in the local language that translates to "restrooms for patrons only."

Sometimes you'll find a collection plate at a toilet, either public or private. Leave a few small coins (often one franc per use) as the or obligation arises. Be sure that you have small change available—no change is given out.

If there are toilets in the area, look for these signs: Toilettes, W.C., Messieurs (Men), Dames (Women).

In a number of markets in open spaces or fields, toilets may be placed in portable trailers. Look for the trailers looming up above the stands. They are often but not always marked.

# Transportation

### Getting to City Markets and Auctions (Weekdays)

The large cities of France have the largest flea markets and usually the largest selection of goods, and are also usually the site of the auction houses. During the week, public transit (subways, busses, and trolleys) may be the the most economical and convenient way to come and go unless you plan to buy and take bulky items away with you.

Most city markets are crowded; parking space is at a premium. Sometimes illegally parked cars are towed, but less frequently if they are out of the path of traffic.

Parking, whether free or pay, whether on the street or in a garage or a lot, is usually found at least several blocks away from the market. Traffic near a market may be almost at a standstill for hours on end. You can usually walk much faster than you can drive.

French subway systems are closed during the early morning hours: during the week they're closed between 11 p.m. or 1 a.m. and about 5 a.m.

A possible middle course is to park further from the market and ride public transit to your destination.

Where information about access via convenient public transit is available, it's included in the description of each flea market.

## Getting to City Markets on Weekends

Weekends call for different preferred modes of transportation to the flea market. The bustle of weekday business and work-related traffic subsides, especially on Sunday. Traffic moves more smoothly and rapidly. Parking is much more easily found, often free, and the tow truck drivers and parking-ticket givers often take the day off.

In contrast, public transit often becomes less convenient. Subways and busses revert to a weekend schedule, offering less- frequent service. Weekend service may be infrequent. On weekends, subways often do not start up until 6 or even 7 a.m., and some stations may close for the entire day. Those at or near flea markets remain open. Sometimes getting to a Sunday market opening on public transit is impossible. Later in the day, service becomes more frequent, but is rarely up to weekday rush-hour frequency.

## Countryside and Suburban Markets

A van or car is almost indispensable for a tour of country markets. Small cities, towns, and villages don't usually have the frequent public transit services found in large cities. Intercity trains don't arrive every five minutes, busses are few and far between, and there are no subways.

French roads are well maintained. Autoroutes (expressways) are well maintained and marked, have high speed limits (maximum 130 kilometers, or about 80 miles per hour). Outside of metropolitan areas, most autoroutes are toll roads, and costs can be high.

Every village is found on the detailed maps published by Michelin. You'll find these maps at bookshops, tourist curio shops, and sometimes gas stations. (Several oil company sell their own maps at gas stations, though most are less detailed.)

## Cars and Vans

Renting a car in France is as easy as in the United States or Canada. All you need is your state or provincial driver's license and a credit card.

France adds a 33 per cent value-added tax (TVA) to the price of car rentals. You can lease tax-free vehicle in France if you keep it for at least 21 days and arrange it in advance.

Rentals and leases can be handled from home, before you leave. In addition to major rental companies such as Avis, Hertz and National, European car rental specialists such as Auto-Europe and Europe-by-Car have offices in the United States and Canada (check for their "800" numbers both in the United States and Canada).

Generally, as a rule of thumb, you can rent a small economy car for less than the cost of two first-class Eurailpasses for the same period of time. There are also potential savings on lodging and meals, if you stop in smaller towns and villages. Central city prices are about one-and-a-half times countryside prices for equivalent quality.

If you buy a vehicle to bring home, it must meet U.S. or Canadian specifications. If you buy a used vehicle in Europe, plan to resell it before you come home,

Vehicles also offer far greater convenience in keeping your finds at hand rather than leaving them at left-luggage offices at train stations.

If several of you travel together, you can search the market independently, and find the car a convenient meeting place. Each one of you should have a key.

## Carrying Your Purchases

When using public transit, you have to carry your purchases with you or send them along by railway express ("service de colis"). Your finds are generally safer when you can carry them with you until you're ready to come home or ship them home.

From this standpoint, a car or van is almost a necessity for serious collectors or dealers on a buying trip. Otherwise, carrying around your treasures can be an exercise of frustration, and cost a fortune in excess baggage, postal, and express shipping charges. Take a hint from the dealers and regular buyers: they don't usually arrive on public transit. They drive.

# Carrying Your Finds at Market

Few sellers have adequate, secure, convenient wrapping materials. Most will just hand you the purchased item, possibly wrapped in an old newspaper. Once in a while, a flimsy plastic shopping bag may be available if you ask. These bags are better than nothing, but are lightweight, and can stretch or tear if filled with heavy or sharp-pointed objects.

You're best off bringing your own carry bag.

### Selecting a Market Bag

There are a large variety of carry bags available, such as day pack or gym bag. Nylon bags are best: they are strong, light, fold into small places, and shield the contents from the prying eyes of potential thieves. Shoulder straps leave your hands free to inspect items.

Carefully check a bag before you buy it. Look for durability and convenience first rather than style. A good bag has these qualities:

1. The material is strong. Rip-stop nylon is the most durable lightweight fabric. Canvas is heavier (in weight, not strength) and can rot if left in the damp for extended periods.

2. The stitching is strong and seams are secure.

3. The zippers are strong and substantial, and open and close easily.

4. All metal parts are thick and strong: solid brass is best.

If you plan on extensive purchases, take more than one bag with you.

## Luggage Carriers

Tourists at very large markets sometimes bring wheeled luggage carriers. They have a number of limitations that make them less useful there than at airports and train stations. Many flea markets have a lot of barriers to the small wheels, such as dirt, gravel, or uneven cobblestone surfaces. Curbs also may interfere with smooth rolling. Many indoor flea markets have stairs that further reduce the utility of these carriers.

Flea markets and antique fairs by their very nature are very crowded, full of jostling people intent on their business. They don't expect to find luggage carriers in their way, and may trip over them.

If you do use a luggage carrier, be sure it is strong and will take a lot of punishing use without breaking. And be sure that the boxes or suitcases can be firmly fastened to the carrier.

## String Bags

At one time every store and market had inexpensive string bags for sale. They could fit in a pocket, and seemingly expand to endless degree. Now it is often difficult to find them.

While old-fashioned classic string bags are more compact and portable than nylon gym bags, they also reveal the contents to the casual observer, and provide less protection against damage.

# Export Laws and Regulations

### ("Protection of the National Cultural Heritage")

France, like most European nations, regulates and restricts export of antiques and artwork considered to be of cultural value. This is to ensure that the "national cultural patrimony" is not lost to foreign countries. In general, the rare, better known, and older items will not be permitted to permanently leave France. When an attempt is made to illegally export an item, it may be confiscated by French customs. Some nations will under some conditions assist the French government to recover illegally exported items and return them to France. This is generally rare in Canada and almost unheard of in the United States.

Offices in Paris and major provincial cities oversee the rather cumbersome export licensing procedure, which requires approval of the exportation from both French Customs and a museum expert.

### Basic Laws

Beginning early in this century, France has amassed a complex web of laws, decrees, and ordinances regulating the protection and export of art objects, antiquities, and collections.

The basic law of 31 December 1913, Article 14, provides for a schedule (list) of items considered of national cultural importance, whether publicly or privately owned. It gives the government the right to inspect, control movement of, and pre-empt sale of any item which has been scheduled. (Generally, only items of outstanding importance are scheduled—and these almost never come up for sale.)

The law of 23 June 1941 generally imposes the export requirements for scheduled items and also for all items falling into a number of protected categories: furniture made before 1830, art objects made before 1900, and all archeological finds regardless of age.

The Notice to Exporters published in the Official Gazette issue of 27 February 1949 details the method to obtain an export license, which has not been substantially changed (and is detailed below).

Additional Notices to Exporters published 24 November 1964 and 30 October 1965 further defined the categories, and states which customs posts must be used in the export of particular types of articles.

Penalties for failure to attempt export without proper papers can result in confiscation of the work(s) and a fine of twice their value.


## Classes of covered items

Most items may be exported with a proper permit. The following classes of items must have an export license to be exported. They are found in the customs regulations, called "tarif des douanes."

The regulated classifications are:

- Ex 99.01: Pictures, paintings, and drawings made entirely by the artist's hand, unless the artist is still living or has died in the last 20 years.

- Ex 99.02: Original engravings, prints, and lithographs more than 100 years old.

- Ex 99.03: Original sculptures and statues in any material and medium, unless the artist is still living or has died in the last 20 years.

- Ex 99.05: Collections and of botanical, anatomical, and mineral specimens for collections unless they are to be used for instructional purposes. Coins and medals (or collections of them) less than 100 years old are specifically excluded from licensing requirements.

- Ex 99.06: Antique objects, (defined as items over 100 years old) except for musical instruments, books, maps, and all other graphic arts.

You must request an export license for any items or shipment in any of these categories with a combined shipment value of over 30,000 Francs.

A request for the export license must be accompanied by a list of items you want to export, with an estimate of the value of each, and (if possible) a photograph of each.

Requests can be made by you or by an intermediary and must be made to:

SAFICO (Services des autorisations financières et commerciales)
  42 rue de Clichy
  75436 Paris Cedex 09
  Telephone 42.81.91.44.

Before the items may be exported, a double inspection must be made:

First an authorized expert representing the French museum service (Direction des musées de France) must inspect the item. These experts have regular weekly hours when all items must be made available for inspection. The customs office you deal with will tell you the date and location of the museum's inspection office. (In Paris, this is usually on Wednesday afternoons.) The museum officials have six months to decide if an export license should be granted, though usually this decision is made much more quickly. If a license won't be issued, the museum has the right to buy the work, or you may decide to keep it in France.

Second, if export is authorized, you will receive the export license (License d'exportation Modéle 02). Then you must fill out a regular export declaration (Déclaration d'exportation, Modéle 1060), and present both forms with the items at one of the designated specialized customs offices. When inspection has been completed, the items should be exported immediately.

## Forfeiture Tax

When items declared to be worth more than 20,000 Francs are exported, a export tax of 6% of the value must be paid unless:
1. You are a dealer resident in France.
2. You are a non-resident of France.
3. You are the creator of the work of art.

If the value of the shipment is of over 250,000 Francs, you must also ensure that financial arrangements relating to exchange controls are satisfied. Only a bank can arrange this; usually major banks will have specialized offices for this purpose.

If you don't have sales receipts and the value of the shipment is over 250,000 Francs, you must ask for a DS export declaration (Déclaration d'exportation modéle DS), also available from SAFICO.

Further information about exports can be obtained at the following centers (English not always spoken):

Centre de Renseignements
Direction Générale des Douanes et Droits
  Indirects
182 rue Saint-Honoré
75001 Paris
Telephone 42.60.35.90.

(This office is conveniently across the square from the Louvre and Louvre des Antiquaires.)

Centre de Renseignements
Direction Générale des Douanes et Droits
  Indirects
1 quai de la Douane (Boîte postale 60)
33024 Bordeaux Cedex
Telephone 45.44.47.10, poste (extension) 153.

Centre de Renseignements
Direction Générale des Douanes et Droits
  Indirects
41 rue Sala (Boîte postale 2353)
60215 Lyon Cedex 02
Telephone 78.43.01.76.

Centre de Renseignements
Direction Générale des Douanes et Droits
  Indirects
4 quai Kléber
67056 Strasbourg Cedex
Telephone 88.32.48.90, poste (extension) 211.

Information can also be obtained from regional offices of the customs service, but the information will not be as complete and reliable as from the above centers. These are available in most large cities: look in telephone books for the regional customs office ("Direction Régionale des Douanes").

*A special note on purchases from dealers:*

If you buy an antique that you believe will fall under the export regulations from a dealer, and have any suspicion that an export permit will not be granted, you should specify that issuance of an export license is a condition of sale. Naturally, this is difficult if not impossible for items bought at auctions or at flea markets.

# Getting Your
Purchases Home

Once you have your antiques and other items, you need to be able to get them home. How you do this depends on many factors: how much material there is, its weight and volume, and how soon you need or want it. You have several options: you can take your purchases with you as baggage, ship them by mail, package express, air freight, or for large items, in a shipping crate. If of great volume, you can have purchases shipped in a 20-foot, 40- foot, or 45-foot (jumbo) shipping container.

## Bringing Purchases Home with You

### Packing Your Bags

When ready to return home laden with your purchases, you can carry it on the plane as hand luggage or check it as baggage. Remember that your baggage is not insured against loss or damage to precious metals, glass and crystal, money, and jewelry. Therefore, you may wish to consider carrying those items onto the plane.

If you decide to check your valuables as baggage, surround breakables with clothes, and, if available, plastic bubble-pack or Styrofoam packing peanuts and shells. These materials are available from shipping supply merchants (look under "Emballages" in the Yellow Pages). Sometimes you can find these materials in the early morning along sidewalks in retail areas or the Paris garment district (third arrondissement).

Sturdy cardboard boxes provide excellent protection. Cartons made for shipping household goods (available from moving companies) and those made in China for shipping food (available in early morning before trash pickup in front of Chinese restaurants and grocery stores) provide the most protection. Almost as durable are cardboard fruit shipping boxes made in France and Italy (available at open air markets and food stores). Those used for apples are very good in size and durability.

Avoid boxes made of a soft grade of cardboard. If you try to fold a corner of a box flap, and it bends easily, cracks, or tears, don't use that box.

Reinforce every cardboard box, especially at seams and corners, with filament tape. Since this tape is not widely available in France, you may want to take a roll with you. Have a sharp knife to cut it—the tape is extremely strong.

*Baggage Allowances Between Europe and North America*

Checked baggage between Europe and North America is counted on the piece system, rather than strictly by weight. If you return from Europe by air, you are entitled to check two pieces of luggage free and take a carry-on with you onto the plane. Each checked package must have a combined length, width, and height less than 62 inches (1.60 meters) and weigh no more than 70 pounds (32 kilograms). Some airlines limit the second piece of checked luggage to 55 inches (1.50 meters) and 70 pounds (32 kilograms). The limits are enforced sporadically, depending on the airline and the airline counter agent.

Carry-on luggage can weigh up to 70 pounds (32 kilograms), but sometimes some airlines will, on some airplanes, limit the luggage to 22 pounds (10 kilograms). In addition to your carry-on, you can often take your camera, purse, day pack and duty-free shopping bag.

Generally, if your purchases are small items and you travel light, the transatlantic baggage allowance will prove sufficient. However, if you have excess baggage, charges can vary wildly between airlines. If you believe (before you make your reservation) that you'll have excess baggage, find out the charges. If they seem excessive, consider changing to an airline with lower excess baggage charges.

If you are not flying directly from Europe to North America, you can expect to have baggage treated on the European weight-based system (see next section).

### *Baggage Allowances Within Europe*

Airlines in Europe (and, most of the rest of the world) accept baggage strictly on weight. Each first-class passenger is entitled to 66 pounds (30 kilograms) of checked luggage and one carry-on. Each business and coach passenger is entitled to 44 pounds (20 kilograms) of checked luggage and one carry-on.

The strictness with which the rules are applied will vary between different airlines at the same airport, the same airline at different airports, and even between one airline counter agent and the next.

Excess baggage charges are often steep! The rule of thumb is to charge one per cent of the first-class fare to every kilogram (or fraction), even if you're not in a first-class seat.

### Shipment by Mail (Parcel Post)

There is usually a limit of 11 pounds (5 kilograms) per package, and costs are relatively high.

You pack the items yourself, either with your own box or an approved carton sold at the post office.

At the post office, go to the window marked "Colis" (packages). You'll have to complete a small green customs declaration ("Fiche de Douane"), which the clerk will give you. On the declaration, you have to state the contents and the value. In addition, you'll have to pay postage, which varies with the type of contents. (Books and papers have a special reduced rate.)

Expect packages to take one to two months to arrive at their destination.

Parcels for delivery in the United States are inspected by the United States Customs Service at the port of entry and then forwarded to you. If any duty is payable, the post office will bill you the amount of duty, a $5 Customs fee, and a collection surcharge. If the shipment is entirely duty-free, there is no charge.

Canadian Customs and Excise inspects parcels at the port of entry, and assesses duty. You pay any duty when the parcel is delivered.

## Package (Railway) Express

If the package weighs over 11 pounds (5 kilograms), you may ship it by rail to a port, by sea passage, and, in North America, accept delivery from the post office.

Take the package to the "Consigne de Bagage" (Baggage Check) at any main railway station. You will have to fill out a customs declaration ("Fiche de Douane"). Often, smaller stations don't have these forms: get one from a post office.

Delivery takes approximately four to eight weeks. United States or Canadian Customs inspection is the same as detailed above in the "Shipment by Mail" section.

## Air Freight

When you need quick delivery, you can send packages by air freight. When shipping by air freight, your parcel is best packed in a wooden shipping carton.

You can take the parcel to the city check-in terminal in Paris, or directly to the air-freight terminal at the airport. You can also call air-freight shippers, who include pick-up and delivery. (See "Transports Aériens" in the Yellow Pages and look for the word "Frét".)

Costs are higher than surface transport, but delivery is between three days and one week, including Customs clearances.

While air freight is charged by weight, in general the larger and heavier the item, the less the charge per pound will be. The exact cost will vary, often with the category of merchandise the package contains.

If you ship through an air express company, the company will handle United States or Canadian Customs clearance. If you ship with the airline, you can either clear the package yourself or hire a customs broker to perform these formalities.

## Shipping Through Packers/Shippers

If your purchases are too bulky to take with you or ship by parcel post or express, or because of their age or importance to the French national patrimony require permits for export, you'll probably become involved with a packing and shipping company. If you choose to work through a packer/shipper, most of the small but important details will be taken care of.

For large shipments, the packer's and shippers's costs are more than justified by the time and energy saved. There are several types of shipment, but the packer's and shipper's involvement and most of the paperwork will be the same.

Many shippers' services include:
• picking up of merchandise within a metropolitan area (such as Paris or Lyon)
• packing the merchandise in a shipping crate or container,
• preparing care of all export documentation, (customs clearances, bill of lading)
• carrying freight to a French port, and airport, any North American port of entry you designate, or even to the final delivery location.

While to some extent the costs will vary with the shipper, in Paris you can expect to pay in the neighborhood of 18,000 to 25,000 Francs for a 20-foot container and 25,000 to 35,000 Francs for a 40-foot container for pick up in the Parisian region, packing, export documentation (but antiquities permits are an additional charge), and delivery to the port at Le Havre. The differences in costs are often reflected in the pick-up radius, and care taken to cushion the items and to tightly fit them in for minimum shifting during the shipment. Prices from other areas will generally be somewhat higher.

Note: If you have the shipper perform the pick-up, you'll need to provide the shipper with the name and address of every vendor, as well as the invoice for every item. This will ensure that all of the pickups can be scheduled and all items can be accounted for. Pick-up usually can be accomplished within a week to ten days.

## Choosing a Shipper

Shippers can be found in several ways: by discussion with antique dealers, through shippers' and packers' advertisements in the antiques trade press, at shipping offices at major antique shows and fairs, and in the yellow pages under moving ("Déménagements") or transportation ("Transports"). Many shippers have specialties or limitations. Ask carefully and listen to the answers, and obtain competitive bids for the exact same services.

Most reputable shippers will be pleased to quote a price, and specify exactly what the price includes.

You should ask to see the premises where from which the packer operates: some resemble laboratories and specialize in the shipment of fine arts and rare paintings, while others are in run-down warehouses, and fit huge loads of miscellaneous furniture and bric-a-brac into large shipping containers at a lower price.

Ask for references from the shipper before entering a contract: any reputable shipper will have a number of references.

## Crate or Container?

Generally, smaller loads are packed into wood shipping crates. Some are standard size, while others are custom made for particular items. Larger loads are packed into metal shipping containers eight feet high, eight feet wide, with lengths of 20- feet, 40-feet, or 45-feet (jumbo). Since the price between a crate and a container may be small, it may be worth buying cheap items just to fill up a container. Containers are strong and are sealed at the packer's and are generally opened only by customs officials. Crates are more easily damaged and a bit easier to pilfer.

Delivery times are approximately the same for containers of any size. Sometimes crates take longer than containers.

## Air Freight

Smaller, lightweight items of great value are usually sent by air freight. Some shippers, often those specializing in shipping paintings for museum exhibitions, are specialists in this type of shipment.

Air freight, though not cheap, takes only a few days. In addition, air freight insurance is much less that marine insurance. Generally it costs between one and two per cent of the value declared on the invoice, airbill, and customs declaration.

## Shipping By Sea

All international sea shipping companies quote prices in U. S. dollars.

When considering sea shipment, be sure to consider several factors.

Shipping companies are divided into "Conference" lines and "non-Conference" lines. The "Conference" is a price-fixing group of shipping lines. In general, Conference lines charge several hundred dollars more per container, and consist of many of the largest shipping lines with the most frequent shedules.

Non-Conference lines are independents, often working with agents to line up complete cargoes for shipment. Non-Conference lines are more numerous, and service appears to be as reliable as with the Conference lines. The costs are approximately 10 to 20 per cent cheaper than the Conference lines.

The approximate cost to ship to an East Coast port (such as Montréal, Boston, New York, or Baltimore) is: 20-foot container: Conference $1900, non-Conference $1700; 40-foot container: Conference $2300, non-Conference $2200.

The approximate cost to ship to a Gulf port (such as Miami, New Orleans, or Houston) is: 20-foot container: Conference $1900, non-Conference $1700; 40-foot container: Conference $2300, non-Conference $2200. The approximate cost to ship to to a West Coast port (such as Los Angeles, San Francisco/Oakland, Seattle, or Vancouver, B.C.) is: 20-foot container: Conference $2100, non-Conference $2000; 40-foot container: Conference $3200, non-Conference $3050.

If shipping to the West Coast, be sure to specify shipment through the Panama Canal; some shipments have been routed via Houston and truck or rail from there, with delays and damage en route.

When deciding whether to make your own sea shipment arrangements leave or it to your packer, remember that most French packers add a premium (often arount 10 per cent) of the estimated shipping charge to ensure that they don't lose money on currency fluctuations. (This is because the franc-to-dollar rate is calculated at the time it passes mid-point in the ocean rather than at delivery on board the ship.) If you deal directly with the shipping and pay in U.S. dollars, you can usually avoid this premium.

## Marine Insurance

You can purchase two basic types of marine insurance: all-risk, or total-loss. Many importers of less valuable antiques and used items purchase only total-loss insurance, since proving when or how breakage occurred can be difficult if not impossible. However, when shipments of great value are made, the additional cost of all-risk insurance is worth paying. Generally, total-loss insurance costs from one to three per cent of value declared on the bill of lading and customs declaration. All-risk insurance (which covers water damage and damage during port operations, but not damage due to strikes, war, acts of violence, nuclear disaster, or certain other exclusions) costs about twice as much as total loss insurance.

If you choose all-risk insurance, be sure to document the condition of goods shipped before they are packed. Invoices and a photograph of every item are the best proof of condition and value.

## Delivery to the Port of Your Choice

Be sure to specify which port you wish to have as the port of entry in the United States or Canada. Avoid entering the shipment through a distant port: although customs brokers at any port of entry can solve many problems, the farther away the port of entry is from the ultimate destination, the more you'll have to pay for truck or rail shipment inside the United States or Canada.

# Clearing United States Customs

Customs inspection! The very words can strike terror or great amounts of irritation into many travelers: visions of weary inspectors pawing through your luggage in search of contraband are not pleasant, particularly when you have a tight connection to your final destination.

Constitutional protections, such as freedom from arbitrary search or the right to be warned if you're suspected of a crime, don't apply when dealing with any Customs officer at the border. The Customs Service is virtually unique in American government in this regard. The laws relating to the search of vehicles and persons are found in the United States Code at 19 U.S.C.A. Section 482. Case law interpreting this section gives the Customs Service the "broadest possible authority for search." Border searches may be conducted with or without cause.

However, bringing in antiques and collectables can require anything from a simple oral statement of what you bought to what seems to be an almost endless round of paper shuffling and frustration.

If you completely and fully declare every item at the correct price, and make it available for inspection, you shouldn't have to worry.

## What Customs Can Inspect

Every item brought into the United States from any other country must be presented to the U.S. Customs for inspection. The customs inspector, at his discretion, can decide to accept your word and inspect nothing, whether a simple suitcase or an entire shipping container. The inspector can decide for any reason, or no reason, to pull every item out of every package and inspect every item.

The reasons for customs inspection include not only the collection of customs duty but also to ensure that all imports are safe, don't violate copyright or trademark laws, meet varying federal regulations, and are not prohibited (such as narcotics or items made from endangered species).

In general, the procedures fall into two categories: "informal entry" for all shipments whose purchase price or value is less than $1,000, or "formal entry" for all shipments valued over $1,000.

## Informal Entries

Informal entry is the easiest and least time-consuming way to ensure that your purchases quickly pass through customs.

In general, all shipments (whether commercial or for your own use) whose purchase price (including packing but not transportation) is less than $1,000 qualify for informal entry whether with your baggage or sent by mail.

When your purchases accompany you, you can usually use an informal entry. When they are over $400, fill out the simplified declaration form handed out on most planes, ships, and busses. If you're in a car (for example from Canada or Mexico), you can make an oral declaration.

In addition, if the importation is for your own use and is with you as baggage, you can also usually use the informal entry procedure, even when the value of your purchases is over $1000. An oral declaration to the inspector is often sufficient.

In all cases, you should have every bill of sale and receipt readily available to show the customs inspector upon request.

If you have packed goods in boxes, you should have shipping tape, twine, or other materials to reseal the containers when the inspector has finished. While some officers have some tape or other materials available, you can't count on it.

Remember that true antiques are duty free, but the inspector may demand proof. Paintings (but not frames) and many products from underdeveloped nations are also duty free.

## Duty-Free Allowance

If your purchases cost under $400 and you have been outside of the United States for at least 72 hours, you can bring in your purchases duty free as part of your baggage once every 30 days. Duty is assessed at 10% on the next $1,000 of goods. After that, the agent will assess duty as prescribed by regulations: the amount will vary depending on the exact classification of the merchandise. (This exemption is valid only when the items are part of your baggage and you present them in person for inspection.)

## Unsolicited Gifts

You're permitted to send unsolicited gifts duty-free if no more than one package to one individual clears Customs on the same day. The gifts must be worth less than $50. The outside must be clearly marked "Unsolicited Gift—Value under $50". You're not permitted to send these packages to yourself or residents of your house.

## Informal Mail Entries

If you mailed antiques home, obtain a customs declaration form from the foreign post office, complete it, and glue it to the package when you mail it.

Enclose a copy of the invoice inside the package. Customs will inspect the parcel at the port of entry. If duty is payable, the post office will collect the duty and a $5 inspection fee from you when the parcel is delivered to you. (There is no fee for completely duty-free items.)

## Formal Entries

For all commercial shipments entering the United States with a purchase price or value over $1,000, you have to make a formal entry.

Inspectors in some airports may sometimes treat amounts over $1,000 as informal entries when the purchases are part of your baggage. When you're not actually there with the shipment, the formal entry procedure is invariably followed by the Customs Service.

Here are the steps that must take place when your purchases arrive at the port of entry:

1. Provide Customs with an acceptable commercial invoice (as defined in the section on steps to clear Customs), or "pro forma invoice" (an invoice you make up reflecting the actual conditions of the sale; later you will have to provide a commercial invoice).

2. File an Entry Manifest (Customs Form 7533) or other equivalent form (usually taken care of by the shipping company).

3. Complete the Entry Summary (Customs Form 7501).

4. Provide a bond or deposit with the Entry Summary to ensure the payment of duty.

5. Make the goods available for inspection.

6. Pay any estimated payment of duty.

7. Arrange for local delivery of the goods.

If you live near the port of entry and want to oversee each step of the process, you can do it yourself. However, you can also hire a customs broker to handle this process for you.

### Why Hire a Customs Broker?

Customs brokers are licensed and bonded and can handle all of the details of clearing customs if you can't or don't wish to. Naturally they charge a fee for service.

When using a broker, you must still play a part by providing a complete commercial or pro forma invoice and ensure that a complete bill of lading (or airbill) accompanies the shipment. The bill of lading should (if possible) specify the broker who will be clearing the shipment.

Customs brokers cluster around all major ports of entry; they're listed in the Yellow Pages.

The local Customs office often has lists of brokers in the area. However, the Customs staff will not recommend brokers.

## How to Select a Broker

Since there may be at least several dozen brokers near most major ports of entry, you need to carefully select the one that will work best for you. Sometimes antique dealers specializing in imported items will tell you which brokers they use, if any (some dealers take care of this themselves).

Ask these questions of any broker you're considering:

1. What experience do you have with antiques and collectables (or type of merchandise you're importing)? How many shipments of such items have you recently cleared?

2. Can you refer me to several recent customers for whom you have cleared this type of merchandise?

3. How much do you charge? Get a breakdown and ask
• is this fee all inclusive?
• if not, what extra charges can be added?

Some brokers provide all services for a set price, plus the exact amount of any customs duty payable. Others may have a reasonable base price, plus a charge for every single entry they type on forms and every phone call they make or every paper they handle. There is often no relationship between charges and quality of service.

Brokers will commonly charge between $75 and $300 to clear a single shipment, and the value of the shipment often does not have a bearing on the fee.

A knowledgable broker should be able to clear your shipment in just a few days.

## Steps in Clearing Customs (if you do it yourself)

*1. Provide Customs with an acceptable commercial or pro-forma invoice.*

Every formal entry must be accompanied by a commercial invoice. While most of the things that must appear on the invoice are commonplace, the requirements for a complete invoice are spelled out in Federal regulations (1 CFR Title 19, Sections 141.83 (c) and 141.86 through 141.89).

In general, the invoice must state the exact type and quantity of each item, what each type of item is made of, and the price paid (including and specifying whether containers and packing were included). It must also include the name and address of both buyer and seller, and specify the U.S. port of entry. The invoice should be signed or sealed by the exporter. If you have a number of invoices from different sellers, you can combine the items in one shipment. In this case, you can make out a combined invoice, but all of the original invoices should be attached to the combined invoice.

Pro forma invoices can be used to clear Customs but a true invoice must be provided within six months of entry. Otherwise a penalty will usually be assessed out of the customs bond (see below in Section 4).

A special U. S. Customs invoice can be used in place of a regular commercial invoice; contact Customs for more detailed information.

*2. File an Entry Manifest, Customs Form 7533 or other equivalent.*

(This is usually taken care of by the shipping company).

*3. Complete the Entry Summary (Customs Form 7501).*

The Entry Summary form provides, together with the invoice, the basis upon which duty will be determined and assessed.

When filed, it must be accompanied by the invoice, the bill of lading, and bond (or acceptable alternative).

You or your customs broker must complete the form and present it with the rest of the entry documents at the Customs office within five days the shipment's unloading. (While Customs officers may provide information, you or your agent must complete the form, and propose the correct classification for entry.) For exact information to complete the Entry Number, Entry Type Code, Port Code, and similar codes, you will have to contact the regional Customs office.

You must also complete the Description of Merchandise (Items 29-32). This includes not only the description (quantity, value, duty rate, amount of duty payable), but also the tariff classification, which is found in the Tariff Schedule of the United States of America (T.S.U.S.A., usually pronounced "Tsoosuh").

The Entry Summary form must then be signed (press hard—this is a five-part form) and submit these with your Customs bond or equivalent and the invoice.

Using T.S.U.S.A.

This document, usually in the form of a large binder, contains tens of thousands of tariff classifications and rates. What you must do yourself is to determine both the correct classification for the merchandise and the correct rate of duty. Customs officers will not usually tell you what the exact classifications your items fit.

The tariffs are broken down into seven major categories, and then further subdivided. T.S.U.S.A. is available for reference at all Customs offices, major "depository libraries" (usually public or university libraries), or found in bound form in the United States Code Annotated (19 U.S.C.A. Section 1202 and following sections. Related provisions are found in 19 CFR Chapter 1. Both of these are available in large law libraries, or you can buy a copy from the:

United States Government Printing Office
Washington, D. C. 20402


*4. Provide a bond or deposit with the Entry Summary to ensure the payment of duty.*

This must be submitted even if you believe the goods are duty free. The purpose of the bond is to ensure the correct payment of duty.

Customs bonds must be issued by an approved customs bonding company. The local customs office will have a list of local bonding companies. (Most customs brokers include the bonding with their other services.)

The amount of a single entry bond varies, but is generally the value of the shipment and the estimated amount of duty.

A customs bond can be issued either on a permanent basis for importers on a regular basis, or as a single entry bond for a single shipment.


Alternatives to a Customs Bond

There are several alternatives to a customs bond, but they are less convenient. They include:
- A cash deposit equal to the value of shipment (no interest is paid and the cash is held for two years).
- Personal surety (requiring two signatories with real assets in the state in which the port of entry is located).
- Treasury bills, notes or bonds (but not U. S. Savings Bonds) which will also be held for two years, but you eventually receive the interest.

The bond or its alternative must be presented to Customs when you present the invoice and Entry Summary (Customs Form 7501).


*5. Make the goods available for inspection.*

Usually shipments are held in a customs warehouse at the port of entry for up to 10 days. During this time, the inspection should take place. Under certain circumstances, the shipment can also be shipped in bond to a more convenient place (usually a bonded warehouse), or opened in the presence of a Customs officer.

*6. Pay the estimated payment of duty.*

You already have estimated the amount of duty (at the rate found in T.S.U.S.A.) and included it on the Summary Entry form. Make payment of any amount needed; the goods won't be released until the estimated duty is paid.

Rates of Duty

From the thousands of rates found in T.S.U.S.A., most of the ones needed by antique dealers and collectors are here:

All antiques (defined as certifiably at least 100 years old) enter the United States duty free.

All paintings made entirely by hand are duty free, regardless of age (but you may have to pay duty on the frame and packing).

All sculptures made and signed by a "recognized" artist in an edition of 10 or fewer (usually a photocopy of an entry in a bibliography of art and artists will suffice).

Items that are old but do not qualify as antiques are assessed duty as found in T.S.U.S.A.; duties on most items are much lower than you might expect, in the neighborhood of free to about 8 per cent. Naturally exceptions exist, and depend not only on the item but also where it was made or acquired. Duty is imposed based on the classification of the merchandise and its country of origin. In general, imports from France recieve the "most favored nation" rate.

*7. Arrange for local delivery of the goods.*

When you have paid the estimated duty, you are able to pick up or have your goods shipped to their final destination.

While for most purposes, the procedure is finished when you pay the duty, Customs has 90 days to review the paperwork and finalize the transaction. The entry (shipment of merchandise) is completed in 90 days; at that time the entry is "liquidated" (the paperwork is considered final by Customs).

# Clearing Canadian Customs

Customs inspection! These words make many people a bit nervous, and can strike terror in some people. However, when entering Canada, a full and truthful declaration of merchandise will speed re-entry of both you and your purchases. If your purchases are shipped, you'll have to clear them through Customs and Excise yourself or hire a customs broker. Depending on where the merchandise enters Canada and how much there is, clearing customs can require anything from a simple declaration to the customs officer to a formal entry, with all of the paperwork that that may entail.

## What Customs Can Inspect

Every item brought into Canada from any other country must be presented to Customs and Excise for inspection. The customs officer can, at his discretion, accept your declaration or open and inspect any and all portions of the shipment. In general, procedures fall into two categories: informal clearance of items included in personal baggage that you have with you, or formal clearance for shipments of high value, whether with you or sent separately.

Customs inspections are carried out for the purposes of collection of duty, federal sales tax, excise taxes, and to ensure that imports are safe, don't violate copyright, trademark, or drug laws, and that no items made from endangered species are imported.

## Informal Entries

Once a year, travelers returning to Canada after an absence of at least seven days may import items for personal use without paying duty or federal sales tax to the value of $300. After the first trip abroad, Canadian residents can bring up to $100 duty free with them once every calendar quarter after an absence of at least seven days.

All goods exceeding that amount or for resale are subject to duty and federal sales tax (12 per cent), though some items are exempt from sales tax. Excise tax (usually 10 per cent) is added to some categories of imports as well.

## Mail Entries

If you send a package by mail or package express, it will be inspected by Customs and Excise at the port of entry. The assessment will, in large part, be based on the customs declaration ("Fiche de Douane") you attached in France. Any duty, federal sales tax, and excise tax payable will be collected upon delivery.

## Formal and Commercial Entries

If your goods are for resale, you (or your customs broker) must complete the "Canada Customs Import Entry Coding Form (B3)" or the "Commercial Short Import Entry Coding Form (B8)". These forms are available from any Customs and Excise office at any major port of entry (seaports, land crossings, or international airports). Information is also available from:

Customs and Excise
Revenue Canada
260 Coventry Road
Ottawa, Ontario K1K 2C6
Telephone (613) 993-0534

To make a formal entry, you must fill out every box in the form except those reserved for the duty stamp. The most difficult part to complete is the classification of goods. You must make the declaration based on the classifications in the Tariff Schedules. The Tariff Schedules consist of a large loose-leaf notebook containing thousands of different Tariff Items. The Tariff Schedules can be reviewed at any Customs and Excise office.

You must decide the exact classification under which each item falls (there are thousands). To find the correct classification, you must determine which the correct tariff classification. Some common classifications for antiques and collectables include:

- 69315-1: Articles (other than spirits or wines) produced more than 50 years prior to the date of importation. Antiques are admitted duty free but those less than 100 years old must pay 12 per cent federal sales tax. Antiques over 100 years old are exempt from both duty and federal sales tax. Proof of age is usually required.

- 51900 series: Furniture. There are about seven relevant categories, with duty from 10 per cent to 45 per cent, depending on the exact classification and country of origin. In addition to the tariff, a 12 per cent federal sales tax must be paid.

- 32600 series: Glass. There are several dozen separate tariff categories, with duty rates ranging from free (glass eyes) to 32.5 per cent (carboys and demijohn jugs), plus 12 per cent federal sales tax.

- 36200-1: Sterling or other silverware (except silver plate) and gold, with duty ranging from 7 per cent to 45 percent plus 12 per cent federal sales tax plus 10 per cent excise tax on some items.

- 28700-1: All tableware of china, porcelain, semi-porcelain (such as faience), or white granite, but not including earthenware, with duty rates ranging from free to 35 per cent, plus 12 per cent federal sales tax.

• 28600-1: Earthenware and stoneware, with duty rates ranging from 11.3 per cent to 35 per cent, plus 12 per cent federal sales tax.

*Determining Duty Rates Within a Tariff Classification*

The duty charged depends to a great extent on the country of origin. The Tariff Schedules include five categories: British Preferential Tariff, Most Favoured Nation Tariff, General Tariff, General Preferential Tariff, and U. K. and Ireland Tariff. In general, imports from France are entered under the Most Favoured Nation Tariff.

## Release of Goods

Goods will not be released from Customs and Excise until all duty, and, when imposed, federal sales tax and excise taxes have been paid.

## Customs Brokers

Customs brokers are licensed and bonded and can handle all of the details of customs clearance if you can't or don't wish to. They charge fees for all services they perform.

Customs brokers are found in all major ports of entry, particularly seaports. They are listed in the Yellow Pages under "Customs Brokers."

## How to Select a Broker

Since most ports have at least several brokers, and charges for customs entries are not uniform between one and another, consider several factors before choosing a broker.

Ask these questions of any broker you're considering:

1. What experience do you have with antiques and collectables (or type of

merchandise)? How many shipments of similar items have you recently cleared?

2. Can you provide references of recent customers for whom you have cleared this type of merchandise?

3. How much do you charge? Request a breakdown of fees and ask:
- is this fee all-inclusive?
- if not, what extra services will be incur a charge? And how much are the extra charges likely to be?

Carefully compare brokers' charges and services: some specialize in certain types of imports, and some have fee schedules better suited to certain types of shipments.

# Writing and Calling

## Postal Codes and "Départements"

Every French address has a five-digit postal
code; its use is the same as the zip code in the
United States or post code in Canada. It is
generally written before the name of the town.
The first two numbers of the postal code refer
the administrative "Département," which is
roughly analogous to a county. Most of the approximately 100 départements are named after
natural features (most often rivers and moun-
tains). Therefore, there is no pattern to determine what part of France each département occupies.

## Writing to French addresses

When writing for information, be sure to put the
postal code before the the city name; in large
cities, the postal code changes from area to area,
just as zip codes and post codes change in the
United States and Canada.

When you see "Cedex" as part of an address be
sure to use it. This will send it to a special post
office that has only post boxes.

## Telephone Calls

When making a phone call inside Paris or to or
from any region of France except Paris (whether
local or long distance), just dial the entire eight-
digit number. If you are calling to the provinces from Paris, or from the provinces to Paris,
first dial 16, wait for second dial tone, and
then dial the number.

A complete explanation of using French
telephones is found in "Manston's Travel Key
Europe," available from the publishers of this
book.

## Languages Spoken

Often, the tourist office (Office de Tourisme) will
have English speakers. It is somewhat rarer to

find a fluent English-speaker at local chambers of commerce (Syndicats d'Initiative) have them, since these offices are found in smaller towns. You can't expect that most people you meet at markets, fairs, auctions, offices, and companies will speak English. Generally, younger people recently out of school are most likely to know some English.

## Is the Market Going to Be There?

When markets or auctions are held at least once a month, you can expect to find them at the time and place promised. Checking with the listed organizer or information source is not usually necessary. If markets are held less often, it is important to check in advance to confirm the exact dates.

# Cities A to X

### Agde 34300

Marché de brocante (junk market) every Sunday morning from the beginning of June to mid-September on Quai de la Trinquette and Quai de la Trirème at the Cap d'Agde. The market in this newly- created summer resort is interesting; a couple of dozen vendors bring junk including glass, domestic pottery such as jugs and casseroles, and, if you're lucky, pharmacy pots and old drug bottles. Do not confuse the antique market with the Wednesday food market and the Saturday food and clothes market. Information from the Office Municipal du Tourisme et des Loisirs, Centre des Congrès, avenue des Sergents, Boîte Postale 544, 34300 Cap d'Agde, telephone 67.26.00.97.

### Aigues-Mortes 30220

Foire à la Brocante (junk fair) third weekend of June at the foot of the old city walls at Porte de la Gardette. This ancient town, bypassed by the centuries, is on the edge of the windswept Camargue region. The market has typical items of southern France: old copper basins, farm implements, tack (for horses), and, if you're lucky, painted wooden country items. This is one of the major markets in the south of France. Information from the M. Delmas, Union des Commerçants et Artisans d'Aigues-Mortes, telephone 66.53.73.47.

### Aix-en-Outhe 10160

Marché à la brocante (junk market) second Sunday of every month at Le Mineroy. This small, provincial market in Lorraine is full of country items, organized by a recognized authority and antique dealer. Information from M. Robert Richard, Le Mineroy, 10160 Aix-en-Outhe, telephone 25.46.72.69.

## Aix-les-Bains 73100

Exposition-Vente d'Antiquités (antiques exposition and sale) first Friday through following
Monday in October in the Palais des Fleurs on
rue Jean Monard. This is a small regional sale in
a famous old thermal resort. Information from
the Commission d'Animation du Palais des
Fleurs, rue Jean Monard, 73100 Aix-les- Bains.

## Aix-en-Provence 13100

Marché aux puces (flea market) Tuesday,
Thursday, and Saturday from 8 a.m. to 1 p.m.
year round at the place de Verdun facing the
Palais de Justice. The setting is one of the
most picturesque in France, and the twenty or
thirty vendors of antiques and collectables offer
good variety. This market offers a lot of porcelain
and some faience, much silver and silver plate,
books, and some crystal. There is only a small
quantity of furniture. A few vendors have spilled
over into the adjoining place de Precheurs,
which is mainly a food market. The food
market displays the agricultural plenty of
Provence, especially late in summer, when the
melons from nearby Cavaillon share top billing
with tomatoes and peaches. There are no
toilets at the market. Parking is difficult in
this congested, ancient area. Pay parking
garages are found several blocks away at place
Bellegarde, and also along boulevard Saint-
Louis. Information from the Office du
Tourisme, place Général de Gaulle, 13100 Aix-
en-Provence, telephone 42.26.02.93.

Salon des Antiquaires (antique dealers' salon)
first two weeks of October (exact dates change
from year to year) at the Salle Carnot, 14 place
Carnot. This salon is full of Provençal artisans'
work and a has a good selection of antiques. This
is one of the larger annual markets in the
south of France. Organized by the M. Bouzon,
Syndicat des Antiquaires Aixois, 13 rue
Granet, 13100 Aix-en-Provence, telephone
42.26.02.93 or 42.23.16.86.

## Ajiccio (Corsica) 20000

Marché aux puces (flea market) every Saturday and Sunday morning at the Marché Central (central market hall) right in the center of town along the boulevard du Roi Jérôme facing the city gardens. This lively market, which is part of the general market offering food and new items, mainly offers junk and regional specialties such as copper cauldrons, old armaments left over from the feuding days, and Napoleonic souvenirs. Information from the Office de Tourisme (closed Saturday and Sunday), 38 Cours Napoléon, 20000 Ajiccio, telephone 95.21.55.31.

## Albi 81000

Marché aux puces (flea market) every Saturday morning year round on place Lapérouse, just near the old town center, with its narrow, picturesque, and twisting streets. You may find regional items such as copper basins, folk art, domestic pottery such as plain clay wine pitchers and platters. Parking garages are available in the neighborhood on boulevard Général Sibille, not too far from the cathedral. Information from the Office de Tourisme, 19 place Saint-Cecile, 81000 Albi, telephone 63.54.22.30.

Foire à la brocante et aux antiquaires (junk and antique dealers' fair) first weekend of October. This is a regional fair of between fifty and one hundred dealers. Organized by C.F.E.A., 14 rue Timbal, 81014 Albi, telephone 63.54.67.19.

## Alençon 61000

Salon d'automne d'antiquités et de brocante (autumn antique and junk salon) the end of October and beginning of November. This is a relatively small regional fair, held indoors at the Parc des Expositions. Information from the

Parc des Expositions, Boîte Postale 109, 61004 Alençon Cedex.

## Amboise 37400

Salon d'antiquités (antique salon) during the first two weeks of July (centering on July 14, which is Bastille Day) at the Grange de Négron. This small regional fair doesn't offer large size or distinctive items, but is often crowded with summer tourists. Information from Mme. Huauly, 12 rue Nationale, 37400 Amboise.

## Amiens 80000

Marché aux puces (flea market) every Saturday morning year round at place Henriette Dumin. This market in the level northern region of France is part of the weekly general merchandise and food market. Dozens of vendors turn out on the few sunny days; in inclement weather there are fewer, selling regional specialty items including faience, household copper ware, and beer pitchers and mugs. Information from the Office de Tourisme, Maison de la Culture, rue Jean Catelas, 80000 Amiens, telephone 22.91.79.28.

## Angers 49000

(Please also see Durtal 49430)

Marché aux puces (flea market) Saturday from early morning to about noon year round at place Louis Imbach. The setting is wonderful: quaint old buildings surround this tree-shaded, irregularly shaped square. Though over 100 sellers are at this mixed market, many sell only new items and food. This market has a fair amount of used furniture (less on rainy days) plus normal flea-market items such as glass, crystal, porcelain, tarnished silver plate (and a little solid silver). No public toilets are available. Street parking is difficult, since during the rest of the week the square is the neighborhood parking lot. Information from the Office de Tourisme, place Kennedy, 49000 Angers, telephone 41.88.69.93.

Salle des Ventes (public sales hall) auction every Tuesday at 2 p.m. Information and buyer registration is held before the market begins. Information from Salle des Ventes, 52 rue du Maine, 49000 Angers, telephone 41.60.55.19.

Marché aux fleurs (flower market) every Saturday morning at place Bessonneau, in the central city area. This market sells mostly flowers, not antiques and collectables. Information from the Office de Tourisme, place Kennedy, 49000 Angers, telephone 41.88.69.93.

## Angoulême 16000

Marché aux puces (flea market) first and third Saturday of the month year round at place Francis-Louvel in the center of this fascinating old walled city. This is one of the more interesting regional flea markets, with dozens of vendors. Specialties of the region include copper ware and faience, and rustic farm furniture and implements. Street parking is difficult in the narrow streets, but there is a garage between the flea market and the nearby city hall. Information from the Office de Tourisme, Hôtel de Ville (City Hall), 16000 Angoulême, telephone 45.95.16.84.

Salon des Antiquaires (antique dealers' salon) the first weekend December (may include the last day or two of November) at the Logis de Lunesse. This fair is where many regional dealers show furniture, copper, and faience. Information from M. Fragne, 8 rue Ludovic Trarieux, 16000 Angoulême, telephone 45.95.62.42.

## Annecy 74000

Marché aux puces (flea market) last Saturday of every month year round on flowered banks of the Thiou river in the city center and along the lake. This is one of the most picturesque markets in

France; you may find regional specialty items including wooden butter molds and primitive folk art and wood carving, household items, and occasionally heavy rustic furniture and painted farm furniture. Information from the Service des Affaires Economiques, Boîte Postale 305, 74000 Annecy, telephone 50.52.81.80.

Salon d'antiquités de la rentrée (antique and collectors' salon) at the end of August and first few days of September at the Parc des Expositions. About 100 exhibitors (mainly dealers) display their wares, which include furniture, wood items, and occasional silver pieces. The first two days (always Thursday and Friday) are reserved for dealers—bring your business card and maybe a copy of business license or tax registration certificate). There is no entry fee for dealers, but there is an admission charge for the public. Information from the Parc des Expositions, 74000 Annecy, telephone 50.45.01.04.

Les Antiquaires de l'Emeraude (antique dealers of Emeraud), every day except Sunday and Monday morning at 4 rue Jean Jaurès. This building containing about 25 dealers, offering items such as 18th- and 19th-century furniture, Art Deco knicknacks, lamps, and furniture, and other items. Pay parking is available at place de la Préfecture and also the Parking de Bonlieu (along the avenue d'Albigny).

## Annet 77410

Marché aux puces (flea market) second Sunday of every month year round at 15 rue du Mancel. This is a small flea market near the western edge of the Parisian suburbs. The selection runs to cut glass, crystal, bronzes, and other items usually found in Paris. However, few of the best items are found at this market.

## Annonay 07100

Marché aux puces (flea market) second Sunday of the month year round. This is a small market in a poor area. Prices will be lower than in major cities. and rustic items predominate. Information from the Office de Tourisme, 3 rue Sadi-Carnot, telephone 75.33.24.51.

## Antibes 06600

Marché aux puces (flea market) Thursday and Saturday mornings at the place Audiberti. This is an interesting but relatively touristed market. Organized by Service d'Animation Economique Communale, Halles, et Marchés, Mairie d'Antibes, 06600 Antibes, telephone 93.61.32.37. Information is also available from M. Gismondi, Association des Commerçants du Viel Antibes, 18 place Audiberti, 06600 Antibes, telephone 93.34.65.65.

Salon des antiquaires (antique dealers' salon) two weeks at Easter (the end of March and/or early April) during daylight hours on the yacht harbor's edge at Port Vauban. A large parking lot near the port is free to salon patrons. Information from M. Gismondi, Association des Commerçants du Viel Antibes, 18 place Audiberti, 06600 Antibes, telephone 93.34.65.65.

## Apt 84400

Marché aux puces (flea market) every Saturday morning (early!) at the place des Carmes. This Provençal market is a good one in an area that is a traditional source of antiques and folk art. In particular, you may find local pottery (both glazed and unglazed), jars, jugs, and pots. You may also find old forged iron kettles, fire pokers, or similar items. Once in a rare while you will find old glass truffle jars. Information from the Office de Tourisme, avenue Philippe de Girard, 84400 Apt, telephone 90.74.03.18.

Foire à la brocante (junk fair) last Saturday of July through the following Tuesday in the town center. About 100 private collectors, junk and antique dealers, offering, in addition to normal flea market items, rustic Provençal furniture, possibly even a few minor paintings. Information from the Office de Tourisme, avenue Philippe de Girard, 84400 Apt, telephone 90.74.03.18, or from the organizer, M. Gassier, Boîte Postale 45, 84800 L'Isle-sur-Sorgue, telephone 90.38.10.43.

## Arcachon 33120    (Please see Teich)

## Argenteuil 95100

Marché aux puces (flea market) every Sunday morning year round on boulevard Héloise and the adjoining Promenade Gabriel-Peri. Several dozen vendors offer items such as minor faience and porcelain, bistrot glassware, lamps, milk pitchers, et cetera. Since this market is in a suburb of Paris, expect Parisian quality in the displayed items, and Parisian prices to match.

## Arles 13200

Marché aux puces (flea market) Saturday morning year round from dawn to about noon on boulevard des Lices, and straggling along part way down boulevard Victor Hugo. During the week the wide shoulders of the boulevard are parking lots; on Saturday they sprout hundreds of vendors, mostly of food. This is one of the liveliest markets in France, rain or shine. The dozen to two dozen antique and junk dealers congregate on the small path in the small park leading up to rue Vauban. Only small amounts of furniture are brought to this market, but there is often a lot of good-quality silver plate and crystal. The rest of the market includes squawking caged chickens and cooing doves, vegetable and fruit vendors, and bakers' products including round, domed country breads baked in wood-fired ovens.

Arles is also the center of the olive-wood carving area, though few of these products are found at the market. These graceful free-form bowls are new, becoming scarce, and not cheap, but are not found anywhere else in the world. Public toilets are in the park, but are poorly maintained. Parking is very difficult—plan to park a few blocks away and walk. Information from Mairie d'Arles, place de la République, 13200 Arles, telephone 90.93.98.10.

Salon des antiquaires et de la brocante (antique and junk dealers' salon) last week of September (two weekends and the week between them) from 10 a.m. to 7 p.m. at the Palais des Congrès on the bank of the Rhone river on avenue Président Allende. About 50 dealers bring extensive quantities of antiques, furniture, and collectables to this fair. Information from M. Maurin, 4 rue de Grille, 13200 Arles, telephone 90.96.51.57.

Salon des Antiquaires (antique dealers' salon) last weekend of October and All Saints' Day (a legal holiday) at the Salle des Fêtes on the boulevard des Lices. Organized by Affentranger, 2 Rond-Point des Arènes, 13200 Arles, telephone 90.96.11.92.

## Aubagne 13400

Marché mensuelle de brocante et de l'artisanat (monthly junk and handcraft market) the last Sunday of the month at the Gros de la Tourtelle. This is the largest flea market in the vicinity of Marseille, and is also relatively free of tourists.

## Auch 32000

Marché aux puces (flea market) second Saturday of every month year round at the Maison de Gascogne and market hall across the street from the post office. Information is available from the Syndicat d'Initiative d'Auch, place Cathédrale, 32000 Auch, telephone 62.05.22.89.

Salon des Antiquaires (antique dealers' salon) first 15 days of September at the Maison de Gascogne and market hall across the street from the post office. Here you'll find Gascon specialties such as pottery, copper basins, farm furniture, cast iron ware, and old bottles. This is one of the more interesting markets in southern France. Information is available from the Syndicat d'Initiative d'Auch, place Cathédrale, 32000 Auch, telephone 62.05.22.89.

## Audun-le-Tiche 57390

Marché aux puces (flea market) second Saturday of the month year round in the afternoon only in this small Lorraine town. This market can offer finds such as faience, pine wood carvings, and small furniture.

## Aumale 76390

Foire à la brocante (junk fair) third Sunday of May and third Sunday of October (starts early) at the place des Marchés and adjoining Halle au Beurre, northeast of the town center. This relatively small regional market may yield odds and ends from the north country and Normandy. Information from the Syndicat d'Initiative, rue Centrale, 76390 Aumale.

## Aurillac 15000

Marché aux puces (flea market) first Saturday of the month year round in the Quartier des Alouettes, near the regular food and general market. This market is rather small and unsophisticated, relatively strong on folk art as would be expected in a never- prosperous region in the mountainous center of France. Information from the Office de Tourisme, place Square, 15000 Aurillac, telephone 71.48.46.58.

## Auxerre 89000

Salle des Ventes (public sales hall) auction every Friday at 2 p. m. Expect to see heavy Burgundian furniture (especially from the 19th century) farm tables, faience, rugs, and occasional tapestries, silver tastevins (wine tasting cups), and more. Information and sales at the Salle des Ventes, 21 avenue Pierre-Larousse, 89000 Auxerre, telephone 86.52.17.98.

## Avignon 84000

(Please also see Villeneuve-les-Avignon, just across the river.)

Marché de brocante (junk market) every Saturday year round from 7:30 a.m. to 6 p.m. (closed 12:30 to 2:30 p.m.) at place Crillon, on the Rhone bank, at the main bridge (Pont Edouard Daladier). This market often has local items such as old winemaking items and bottles, local pottery, hand-blown glass, and, very rarely, carved olivewood. Twice a year, the last weekend of May and last weekend of August, the market becomes much larger and spills out along the riverbank Allées des Oulles. Information from the Office de Tourisme, 41 Cours Jean-Jaurès, 84000 Avignon, telephone 90.82. 65.11, or (for the May and October fairs) from the organizer, M. Gassier, Boîte Postale 45, 84800 L'Isle-sur-Sorgue, telephone 90.28.10.43.

Petit marché aux puces (little flea market) every Sunday morning from 8 a.m. to noon at the place des Carmes, east of central square and Palace of the Popes. This fine tree- shaded square faces the Saint-Symphorien Church. The market has about 30 regular dealers. However, finds are less likely than the Saturday market because this market is better known. Information from the Office de Tourisme, 41 cours Jean-Jaurès, 84000 Avignon, telephone 90.82.65.11.

Salon des antiquaires (antique dealers' salon) second week of February at the Palais des Expositions. You will find dozens of dealers from the region and a lot of Provençal furniture. Information from the Office de Tourisme, 41 cours Jean-Jaurès, 84000 Avignon, telephone 90.82.65.11.

Hôtel des Ventes (public sales hall) auction every Thursday at 9 a.m. This is one of the larger regular auction sales; often you can find rustic Provençal armoires, buffets, and marriage chests. This auction hall also has occasional auctions of better-quality, specialized items. Advance catalogues are available, and these special sales are announced in the Gazette de l'Hôtel Drouot. Inspection and buyer registration are held the day before the sale. Information and sales at the Hôtel des Ventes, 74 bis rue Guillaume Puy, 84000 Avignon, telephone 90. 86.35.35.

Additional street markets, which always seem to include a few antique and junk dealers among the vendors of fruit, vegetables, clothes, and other odds and ends are found at:

- avenue Trillade, every Wednesday, outside the south city walls, under and past the railroad tracks along the airport road. Information from the Office du Marchés, Hôtel de Ville, 84000 Avignon, telephone 90.82.99.00.

- Le Rocade, first Wednesday and Sunday of the month. Information from the Office du Marchés, Hôtel de Ville, 84000 Avignon, telephone 90.82.99.00.

- avenue Colchester in the Saint-Jean district every Thursday year round. Information from the Office du Marchés, Hôtel de Ville, 84000 Avignon, telephone 90.82.99.00.

- place J.-P. Rameau every Saturday morning. Information from the Office du Marchés, Hôtel de Ville, 84000 Avignon, telephone 90.82.99.00.

## Barjac 30430

Foires de Barjac (Barjac fairs) Easter Sunday and the following Monday, August 12-15 (Assumption Day holiday) and the Post Card Fair on the first Saturday and Sunday of January after New Years' Day at the Mas de Jurande.

These fairs in the hills of the Midi in south-central France prohibit sales of reproductions. Regional dealers predominate, offering folk art, old copper, and country furniture. These are major fairs and well worth attending. Organized by the Comite d'Expansion, Mas de Jurande, 30430 Barjac, telephone 66.52.42.39.

## Bar-le-Duc 55000

Salon des antiquaires (antique dealers' salon) usually the second week of September. The show is one of the oldest in France; here is a place to find fine 18th-century wooden furniture from the province of Lorraine. Since it is widely announced in the European antique trade press, you'll find buyers from all over northern Europe. Information from the M. Moes, Mairie de Bar-le-Duc, 55000 Bar-le-Duc, telephone 29.79.02.10.

## Bayeux 14400

Salle des Ventes (public sales hall) auctions every Saturday (occasionally also on Sunday) at 2:30 p.m. Public inspection and buyer registration is the morning of the sale. Street parking is difficult; there are two pay lots at the end of the street. Information and sales at the Salle des Ventes, 7 rue des Bouchers, 14400 Bayeaux, telephone 31.92.04.47.

## Bayonne 64100

Marché aux puces (flea market) every Friday from 6 a.m. (really!) to 2 p.m. at the Halles Municipales on place d'Aine. Several dozen vendors are always at this market, which is far larger on the first Friday of every month. You won't find much furniture (since much Basque furniture consists of massive armoires, farm tables, and marriage chests) but there's a good amount of faience from Samadet, and locally fired clay jugs for water and oil. Information from the Office de Tourisme, place Liberté, 64100 Bayonne, telephone 59.59.31.31.

## Beaune  21200

Salon des Antiquaires et Brocanteurs (antique
and junk dealers' salon) last weekend of March
or first weekend of April. This is a regional fair
of about 50 or 60 dealers. Expect to find heavy
Burgundian provincial furniture, and silver tastevins (small wine tasting cups). Organized by
M. Dubois, 5 avenue de Genève, 74160 Saint-
Julien-en-Genevois, telephone 50.49.27.40.

Village des Antiquaires (antique dealers' village)
open every day except Sunday at 21 boulevard
Saint-Jacques. Ten dealers have permanent
shops in this indoor arcade and charge high
prices for furniture, art objects, etc. These merchants give sizable trade discounts to dealers;
bring a business card or copy of a business
license. Information from the same address,
telephone 80.22.61.30.

## Belfort 90000

Marché aux puces (flea market) first Sunday of
every month year round in the city center. This
is a relatively small market in the southeast of
France. Since local cultural influences are from
neighboring Alsace and Franche-Comte, you'll
find items from both areas, but there don't seem
to be many local specialties. Organized by the
Ville de Belfort Service des Marchés, Hôtel de
Ville, place d'Armes, 90000 Belfort, telephone
84.28.12.23.

Salon des antiquaires et brocanteurs (antique
and junk dealers' salon) third weekend of June
at the Patinoire (ice skating rink). This is the
only regional fair in the area. Organized by M.
Dubois, 5 avenue de Genève, 74160 Saint-
Julien-en-Genevois, telephone 50.49.27.40.

## Besançon 25000

Petit marché a la brocante (little junk market) every Friday and Saturday morning year round (better on Saturday) at the place de la Revolution in the center of town in front of the entrance to the fine arts museum (which has an excellent collection of clocks and time pieces). The antique section of this food and general-items market has only about half-a-dozen vendors, who offer many reproductions and few antiques.

Marché aux puces (flea market) second Sunday every month year round at the Parc des Expositions on rue du Docteur-Mouras, about three kilometers out of town along Route Nationale 73, almost at the bypass road in the Saint-Ferjoux district. This is the best flea market in the area, with about 40 vendors. You'll find watches, clocks, arms, and, somtimes, exquisite fruit-wood carvings and massive copper cauldrons. Information from the Parc des Expositions, Boîte Postale 1913, 25020 Besançon Cedex, telephone 81.52.73.53.

Salon Comtoise des Antiquaires (Franche-Comte antique dealers' salon) first week of October from about 10 a.m. to 8 p.m. at the Parc des Expositions. This is on rue du Docteur- Mouras, about three kilometers out of town along Route Nationale 73, almost at the bypass road in the Saint-Ferjoux district. This is one of the major antique shows of France, with around a hundred dealers showing exquisite clocks, jewelry, and furniture. An admission fee is charged, but there is ample parking on the grounds. Information from M. Coudurier, Parc des Expositions, Boîte Postale 1913, 25020 Besançon Cedex, telephone 81.52.21.74, or from the organizers, Groupe des Salons Selectionées, boulevard de Champagne, Boîte Postale 108, 21003 Dijon Cedex, telephone 80.71.44.34.

## Bergerac 24100

Marché aux puces (flea market) first Sunday of every month year round. This small market is held as part of the much larger Sunday food and general market. Information from the Office de Tourisme, 97 rue Neuve d'Argenson, 24100 Bergerac, telephone 53.57.03.11.

## Béziers 34500

Marché aux puces (flea market) Friday morning (early!) year round at place de 14-Juillet (Champ de Mars). The market site is about 500 meters east of the Allées Paul Rocquet; go on avenue George Clemenceau to the post office, and then turn right at that corner and go for one block. The market is at the end of the block. Parking can be difficult. This is one of the better markets in the south of France: sometimes you can find 19th- century glass, jewelry, and silver (or silver plate), old pharmacy pots and medicine jars, wine-growing tools, and other odds and ends. This is a long-established market, located in a large enough city to have a good selection. Information from the Office de Tourisme, 27 rue Quatre-Septembre, 34500 Béziers, telephone 67.49.24.19.

Salon des antiquaires (antique dealers' salon) twice a year the first Friday through Sunday of February and the first weekend of December, at Mazeran, 3 kilometers from the city center on the Route de Pézenas, to the northeast. This is a strictly local and regional fair, with mainly regional items for sale. Around 70 to 100 dealers participate. Parking is available at the fair site. Organized by M. Salin, S.A.B.P., Route de Pézenas, R.N. 113, 34500 Béziers, telephone 67.30.60.61.

## Blois 41000

Marché aux puces (flea market) first Thursday of every month year round at place Ave-Maria.

This market brings some of the better items of the central Loire valley, including massive copper, rustic faience ware, old muskets, powder horns, and other hunting items, and glassware. The market is moderate in size; only sometimes will you make a find. Information from the Office de Tourisme, 3 avenue Jean-Laigrette, 41000 Blois, telephone 54.74.06.49.

## Bolbec 76210

Salle des Ventes (public sales hall) auction two Saturdays per month (call for exact dates), starting at 2 p.m. Inspection of merchandise and buyer registration in the morning before the sale. You're likely to find large, heavy, dark provincial furniture favored in Normandy, cider mugs, glassware of the 19th century (both cut and painted), and more. Information and sales at the Salle des Ventes, 37 rue Gambetta, 76210 Bolbec, telephone 35.31.06.53.

## Bordeaux 33000

Marché à la brocante (junk market) Tuesday through Friday from 8 a.m. to 6 p.m. and Sundays and holidays from 8 a.m. to about 1 p.m. at place Meynard in the Saint-Michel district, south of the city center. This market is part of a large food and general market; all of the vendors are full-time dealers. Parking is difficult but available at the market halls. Information from the Office de Tourisme, 12 cours 30-Juillet, 33000 Bordeaux, telephone 56.44.28.41.

Marché à la brocante (junk market) Saturday morning year round at place Saint-Pierre, in the old city center not far from the river. Several dozen vendors offer antiques, junk, and modern crafts and sometimes modern art. Information from the Office de Tourisme, 12 cours 30-Juillet, 33000 Bordeaux, telephone 56.44.28.41.

Hôtel des Ventes (public sales hall) auction every Thursday year round at 2:30. Inspection of sale items and buyer registration is held before the auction begins. Information and sales at the Hôtel des Ventes, 46 cours du Médoc, 33000 Bordeaux, telephone 56.39.28.68.

Salon des antiquaires Bordeaux-Lac (Bordeaux antique dealers' salon) second week of February at the Parc des Expositions, about 3 kilometers north of the city center on the main through highway leading to the Pont d'Aquitaine suspension bridge. Several hundred exhibitors show fine antiques, including 18th- and 19th-century paintings, sculpture, silver, and elegant furniture as well as wine paraphernalia. Information from the M. Goulignac, Salon des Antiquaires du Sud-Ouest, 6 rue des Remparts, 33000 Bordeaux, telephone 56.81.80.88.

Salon des antiquaires de Bordeaux-Lainé (Bordeaux antique dealers' salon) in mid-January at the Lainé-Bordeaux warehouse. Information from the Chambre Syndicate des Antiquaires et Brocanteurs, 15 rue Bouffard, 33000 Bordeaux, telephone 45.44.26.64.

## Bourg-en-Bresse 01000

Foire à la brocante (junk market) third Saturday of every month at the fairgrounds at the corner of avenue Maginot and avenue du Champ de Foire. On other Saturdays this is strictly a food market. Place Carriat, which holds the overflow, is cater- corner to the fairgrounds.

Salon des antiquaires (antique dealers' fair) second and third week of September at the Parc des Expositions et de Loisirs at the Ronde Point de l'Ain. Information (and exact dates) from the Parc des Expositions, route de Pont d'Ain, 01000 Bourg-en-Bresse, telephone 74.22.12.33.

## Bourges 18000

Marché de la brocante (junk market) second Sunday of the month from April to November. This is a small market whose location is changeable. Information from the Maison de Tourisme, 14 place E. Dolet, 18000 Bourges, telephone 48.24.75.33.

Journées de l'Antiquité (antique days) the second weekend of February at the Parc des Expositions near the canal. This is not a gigantic fair, is held indoors. A large parking lot is on the site. Information from the Service des Manifestations Commerciales, Maison de Tourisme, 14 place E. Dolet, 18000 Bourges, telephone 48.24.75.33.

## Brest 29200

Marché aux puces (flea market) every Saturday year round from 9 a.m. to 7 p.m. at the Halles de Recouvrance, across the river from the city center on the floating bridge (Pont Mobile) about 800 meters, then right on rue Saint- Exupéry one block to the market hall. This market is part of the general market; most vendors are selling food. This is one of the few flea markets in the picturesque and old-fashioned province of Brittany. There are numerous maritime articles, folk and religious art (especially in wood). Occasionally some good items show up in this market at relatively modest prices. Information from the Office de Tourisme, place Liberté, 29299 Brest, telephone 98.44.24.96.

## Brive-la-Gaillarde 19100

Marché aux puces (flea market) first and third Tuesday of every month year round on Cours Martignac. The market is small and the choice is very limited. Information from the Office de Tourisme, place 14-Juillet, 19100 Brive-la-Gaillarde, telephone 55.24.08.80.

Salle des Ventes (public sales hall) auction every Saturday year round at 2 p.m. Inspection and buyer registration is held before the sale. Information and sales at the Salle des Ventes, 7 rue Vincent-Chassaing, 19100 Brive-la-Gaillarde, telephone 55.24.11.12.

## Caen 14000

Marché aux puces (flea market) first Saturday of the month year round from 7 a.m. until about 1 p.m. at La Petite place and adjoining rue de Vaugueux, right under the battlements of the chateau. In the same neighborhood is the large food and small animal market, which adds color and interest. Organized by Service des Droits des Plans, Mairie de Caen, place Guillard, 14000 Caen, telephone 31.86.48.25, poste (extension) 43.31, or information from the Office de Tourisme et Accueil de France, place Saint-Pierre, 14000 Caen, telephone 31.86.27.65 (English spoken).

Salon des Antiquaires (antique dealers salon) second weekend to third weekend of June, including both Saturdays and both Sundays at the Palais des Expositions. This is one of the major regional shows; you will find many Normandy antiques of all types. A fee is charged for entry. Information from M. Vermughen, C.O.M.E.T., Boîte Postale 6117, 14004 Caen Cedex, telephone 31.73.01.01.

## Calais 62100

Salle des Ventes (public sales hall) auctions every Friday and Sunday at 2:30 p.m. In addition to furniture, this auction offers specialty items of the region such as faience, milk jugs, and old glass items. Inspection and buyer registration is held before the sale. Information and sales at the Salle des Ventes, 24 rue Delaroche, 62100 Calais, telephone 21.97.33.76.

## Cannes 06400

Marché de la brocante (junk market) Saturday from 8 a.m. to 6 p. m. on the the walks at the far end of avenue d'Antibes, which is a continuation of rue Félix Faure, the main shopping street. The market also extends to the shore boulevard near the yacht harbor at Allées de la Liberté opposite the old castle. The selection is best early in the morning. During summer there are more vendors, variety is larger, but the prices are also higher, and there are more tourists. Information from M. Luce di Goianni, 5 boulevard du Moulin, 06400 Cannes, telephone 93.99.22.50.

## Castres 81100

Marché aux puces (flea market) every Saturday morning at place d'Albinique, at the beginning of the road to Albi. The market is part of the general merchandise and food market; only a couple of dozen vendors sell regional items such as pottery pitchers, folk carving, and local faience. Information from the Office de Tourisme, place République, 81100 Castres, telephone 63.35.74.57.

## Chalon-sur-Saône 71100

Petite marché aux puces (little flea market) every Friday year round at rue du Decteur-Mauchamp. This small market of not more than 20 vendors in an unremarkable town can sometimes yield interesting items such as glassware, small clay pitchers and pots, and the small silver (or more usually silver plate sometimes at solid silver prices) "tastevins," used for winetasting. Information from the Office de Tourisme, Square Chabas, boulevard République, 71100 Chalon sur Saône, telephone 85.48.37.97.

Salle des Ventes (public sales hall) auction ever Thursday and Saturday at 2 p.m. This market is often a good place to find massive Burgundian armoires and buffets. Buyer registration and inspection of items are held most work days and the morning of the sale. Information and sales at the Salle des Ventes, 4-6 rue du Temple, 71100 Chalon-sur-Saône, telephone 85.48.10.47.

## Chalons-sur-Marne 51000

Marché aux puces (flea market) last Sunday of the month year round, starting at about 7 a.m. in summer and 8 a.m. in winter at the place du Marché right in the city center. This city, unremarkable except for the soaring cathedral (visible for miles in the open countryside), is a good source of folk art and farm furniture and especially 19th- century odds and ends. About 50 vendors attend this market, which is held indoors. Information from the Office de Tourisme, square Chabas, 51000 Chalons-sur-Marne, telephone 85.48.37.97.

Salon des Antiquaires (antique dealers' salon) first week of April at the Hall des Expositions on avenue du Président Roosevelt. An admission fee is charged; about 80 dealers attend. This show is mostly regional in scope, but is worth visiting. Organized by M. Robert Richard, Le Mineroy, 10160 Aix-en-Outhe, telephone 25.46.72.69.

## Chambéry 73000

Marché à la brocante (junk market) second Saturday of every month at place du Palais de Justice, near the public market halls on rue J. P. Veyrat. This market is of fair size with about 25 vendors in summer and at least 15 in winter. You'll probably see such rustic items as ox yokes, horse collars, cream pots and milk cans, but not too much furniture, crystal, jewelry, or silver. Information from the Office de Tourisme, 24 boulevard de la Colonne, 73000 Chambéry, telephone 79.33.42.47.

Salon des antiquaires et brocanteurs (antique and junk dealers' salon) third week of May at the Parc des Expositions. The first two days are reserved for dealers—take your business card and a copy of your business license. This is a large regional market; you'll find rustic furniture as well as refined items brought by some dealers from Lyon. Information from the M. Cohen, Foire et Salons de Savoie, Parc des Expositions, avenue du Grand Arietaz, 73000 Chambéry, telephone 79.62.22.80.

## Charleville-Mézières 08000

Petit marché aux puces (little flea market) every Tuesday, Thursday, and Saturday at the picturesque place Ducale. This small market is part of the regular outdoor market in a relatively uninteresting town near the Belgian border. Information from the Office de Tourisme, 2 rue Mantoue, 08000 Charleville-Mézières, telephone 24.33.00.17.

## Charmes 88130

La Foire Vosgienne des Brocanteurs (Vosges regional junk dealers' fair) last Saturday and Sunday of September at Xaronval. This is a medium-sized regional fair, where you may find old country furniture, etc. Several dozen dealers from the region sell at this fair. Information from M. Maurice LaCourt, Xaronval, 88130 Charmes, telephone 29.66.12.41.

## Chartres 28000

Foire de la brocante (junk market) fourth Sunday and Monday of the month from May through October at the Saint Pierre church square, early morning to just after noon. This church is southeast of the cathedral down near the river. This market isn't particularly interesting, and usually has a one or two dozen lackluster sellers of small items. One shopkeeper on the square opined that Chartres is too close to Paris and too small a city to retain the best items. Free parking is available on nearby streets. Organized by the Ville de Chartres, 28019 Chartres, telephone 37.21.03.66.

Hôtel des Ventes (public sales house) auctions Tuesdays and Sundays at 2 p.m. Miscellaneous odds and ends, including jewelry, musical instruments, and old photographs and photographic equipment are sold in rapid-fire order. The inspection period is the morning before the sale. Information and sales at the Hôtel des Ventes, 1 bis place Général de Gaulle, 20000 Chartres, telephone 37.36.04.33.

Foire d'antiquaires (antique dealers' fair) last Friday through following Monday of October at the Collégiale Saint-André, just two hundred meters downhill toward the river from the Cathedral. Organized by M. Pigier, Comité Saint-Pierre, 20 rue de la Tonnellerie, 28000 Chartres.

## Chateaubriant 44110

Salon des antiquaires (antique dealers' salon) first part of December. This is a regional market of only modest interest; about 50 dealers offer Breton and Norman antiques. Organized by Prom'Art, 4 rue Offenbach, 35100 Rennes, telephone 99.50.74.19.

## Chateauroux 36000

Marché aux puces (flea market) first Sunday morning of the month from October through June on avenue des Marins in the Quartier des Marins, near and slightly west of the town center. Information from the Office de Tourisme, place de la Gare, 36000 Chateauroux, telephone 54.34.10.74 (closed Sunday and Monday).

Salle des Ventes (public sales hall) auction every Thursday at 2 p.m. Inspection of merchandise and buyer registration is held before the sale. Information and sales at the Salle des Ventes, 5 rue Lemoine-Lenoir, 36000 Chateauroux, telephone 16.34.11.06.

## Chatou 78000

(Please also see Paris.)

Foire nationale à la brocante (national junk fair) beginning of March and end of September, on the Ile de Chatou, near Paris. This is one of the largest antique and junk fairs in France, and is well worth attending. Hundreds of dealers (few private vendors) show all kinds of items. Only truly genuine articles may be displayed and sold at this fair. Everything from statues to crystal, clocks, silver and silver plate, furniture, and nearly anything else can be found at this fair. Access from Paris by public transit to the RER Chatou station, then walk. The four days before the official opening is reserved for the antiques trade: bring your business card and maybe a copy of a business license or sales tax certificate with you to get in. Organized by the French antiques trade association, S. N. C. A. O. (Syndicat National du Commerce de l'Antiquité et de l'Occasion), 18 rue de Provence, 75009 Paris, telephone 47.70.88.78.

## Chinon 37500

Salle des Ventes (public sales hall) auction every Monday at 2 p. m. Merchandise inspection and buyer registration is held before the sale. Information and sales at the Salle des Ventes, 57 rue du Faubourg Saint-Jacques, 37500 Chinon, telephone 47.93.12.64.

## Clermont-Ferrand 63000

Clermont-Ferrand, which among other claims to fame is the home of the Michelin tire company, has several markets that move around the city and immediately adjoining suburbs. As a result, all three are listed here, out of alphabetical order. All of the markets are similar in content, since many of the sellers (both dealers and private parties) move from one to the other.

Marché aux puces (flea market) first Sunday of
every month except May, August, and November
and also on May 11, August 13, and and November 9 from 8 a.m. to 6 p.m. at place 1re. Mai, a
large square and recreation area north east of
the city center near the Michelin factories.
Take avenue de la République to the rue de
Chanteranne. You'll come to the market on the
right before the end of the first block. This
market offers regional furniture of Auvergne,
such as rustic furniture, local faience, jewelry,
and glass, and all kinds of bric-a-brac. Information from the Office de Tourisme, 69 boulevard
Gergovia, 63000 Clermont-Ferrand, telephone
73.93.30.20.

**Montferrand 63100**
(A suburb of Clermont-Ferrand.)

Marché aux puces (flea market) first Wednesday
of every month year round at the place des
Arènes, about four kilometers northeast of the
center of Clermont-Ferrand. This is one of the
larger regional markets of central France. You're
likely to see rustic faience and domestic pottery
such as wine pitchers and oil jugs. Information
from the Office de Tourisme, 69 boulevard Gergovia, 63000 Clermont-Ferrand, telephone
73.93.30.20.

**Royat 63130**
**(A suburb of Clermont-Ferrand.)**

Marché aux puces et antiquités (flea and antique
market) third Saturday of every month on rue
Nationale, right in the center of the old part of
town. About 100 vendors prevent through traffic.
Specialty items include Avergnat wickerwork,
baskets and furniture, old cauldrons of iron or
copper, and, rarely, local faience. This market
is the most picturesque in the region, and is located in the business district of this formerly
fashionable health spa and resort. Information
from the Syndicat d'Initiative, place Allard,
63130 Royat, telephone 73.35.81.87.

## Colmar 68000

Marché aux puces (flea market) first and third Friday of every month from 8 a.m. until 7 p.m. at place de l'Ancienne Douane in the city's central area. This market is far larger in summer when the weather is better and the tourists more plentiful than in winter. Items at this market show Alsace's mixed French and German heritage. Look for vineyard and wine trade items, faience in multicolor on a blue ground, pottery, etc., and occasional pieces of country furniture. (Do not get this market mixed up with the regular Thursday morning market, which takes place until noon, and is one of the more colorful street and food markets in France.) Organized by the Service de la Police Administrative, Ville de Colmar, 6 rue du Chasseur, 68000 Colmar, telephone 89.41.02.29.

Salon des antiquaires (antique dealers' salon) first weekend of May beginning the previous Wednesday and continuing until the following Monday, at the Parc des Expositions. This is a good but not grand show, with about 100 vendors, all of whom are dealers. Information from the M. Busche, Parc des Expositions, avenue de la Foire-aux-Vins, 68000 Colmar, telephone 89.41.60.00.

## Compiégne 60200

Salon des antiquaires (antique dealers' salon) second Thursday through second Sunday of September at the Salle Saint-Nicholas on the rue du Grand-Ferre. This show, about 80 kilometers from Paris, makes a good day trip. About 100 vendors are at this show. Information from the Office de Tourisme, rue de l'Hôtel de Ville, 60200 Compiégne, telephone 44.40.01.00.

## Contrexéville 88140

Salon des antiquaires et brocanteurs (antique and junk dealers' salon) first weekend of September at the Maison de la Culture in this turn-of-the-century thermal resort. The salon is small and of only local interest. You will probably find massive pine and inlaid marquetry fruit-wood furniture, old dental instruments, and lead toy soldiers. Information from the Office de Tourisme, Galeries du Parc Thermal, 88140 Contrexéville, telephone 29.08.08.68, or from the organizer, M. Dubois, 5 avenue de Genève, 74160 Saint-Julien-en-Genevois, telephone 50.49.27.40.

### Corbielle-Essones (Evry) 91110

Foire à la brocante (junk fair) Ascension Day (August 15) on Allée Aristide Briand, one block northwest of the main shopping street, rue Féray. This open-air market is large and traditional, with all kinds of junk. Prices are Parisian, which means higher than in distant provinces. Information from the Office de Tourisme, Syndicat d'Initiative, place de l'Agora, Boîte Postale 16, 91110 Evry, telephone 64.96.23.97.

### Crevecoeur 60800

Marché aux puces (flea market) early morning from early morning to late afternoon on the second Thursday of August (Assumption Day) at place de l'Hotel-de-Ville. This market has taken place for many years, and is a true celebration. Antiques and collectables are interesting, but there are few regional specialties.

### Crozon 29160

Foire à la brocante (junk fair) the first week of April in the town center. This small town has one of the better fairs in Brittany. Organized by Prom'Art, 4 rue Offenbach, 35100 Rennes, telephone 99.50.74.19.

## Cusset 03300

Salon des antiquaires et de la brocante (antique and junk dealers' salon) four days (including the weekend) during the second week of July at the Parc du Chambon. This is a large regional fair. Information from the Comité des Fêtes, Syndicat d'Initiative, Mairie, rue Constitution, 03300 Cusset, telephone 70.98.77.68.

## Dax 40100

Marché à la brocante (junk market) first Thursday of every month year round at the place du Marché Couvert in the center of town near the cathedral. This small regional market is part of the general market; a couple of dozen vendors sell rustic items and junk. Little in the way of silver or art objects is at this market—it is more likely you'll find practical items such as butter molds, stoneware and pottery crocks, and old basins. Information from the Office de Tourisme, place Thiers, 40100 Dax, telephone 58.74.82.33.

## Deauville 14800

Salle des Ventes (public sales hall) auction every Saturday from 10 a.m. until noon and from 2 to 7 p.m. Inspection of merchandise and buyer registration is held before the sale begins. Information and sales at the Salle des Ventes, 16 rue du Général Leclerc, 14800 Deauville, telephone 31.88.21.92.

## Dieppe 76200

Salle des Ventes (public sales hall) auction every Saturday year round at 12:30 p.m. In this seaside town in Normandy, you'll often find nautical items as well as provincial furniture, domestic pottery, and glassware. Inspection of merchandise and buyer registration takes place the day before and on the morning of the sale. Information and sales at the Salle des Ventes, 53 rue de la Barre, 76200 Dieppe.

## Dijon 21000

Marché aux puces (flea market) Tuesday and Friday year round from early morning until just after noon on rue de Soissons and the adjoining place de la Banque. Approximately two dozen vendors offer junk, a few antiques, and, appropriate to the home city of one of Europe's oldest universities, books. The market is only a small part of one of the most exciting street markets in France, which centers on a century-old cast iron market hall reminiscent of the now-vanished Les Halles in Paris. The cast of hundreds selling of food and gadgets lure thousands of customers. Public toilets for 1 franc are available at the market hall. Street parking is difficult, since the market streets are closed to autos, and the most of the narrow central streets prohibit street parking. Pay parking garages are available on rue de la Préfecture, or under the place Grangier.

Salon des antiquaires et de la brocante (antique and junk dealers' salon) every May at the Parc des Expositions et des Congrès, in the northeast part of the city. This is one of the larger regional sales in France, with a particularly good selection of heavy provincial furniture. A small admission charge is made. Toilets are available. A large parking lot is across the boulevard de Champagne. A large flea market takes place in mid- September at the same site. Information from the M. Gonnet, Parc des Expositions et Congrès de Dijon, Boîte Postale 108, 21 003 Dijon Cedex, telephone 80.71.44.34.

Salle des Ventes (public sales hall) auctions every Wednesday and Sunday at 2 p.m. You can inspect the items to be sold and register as a buyer on the morning of the sale. Information and sales at the Salle des Ventes, 44 rue de Gray (near the place du 30 Octobre on the east side of town), 21 000 Dijon, telephone 80.73.17.64.

## Dives-sur-Mer 14160

Marché aux puces (flea market) last Sunday of
the month year round beginning about 8 a.m. on
at the town market hall a block north the rue
Gaston Manneville (the road to Lisieux) at the
church. There are far fewer tourists in winter
than in summer, since this town is adjacent to
the summer beach resort of Cabourg. Information from the Office de Tourisme, Jardins de
Casino, 14390 Cabourg, telephone 31.91.01.09

## Divonne-les-Bains 01220

Grande foire aux antiquaires et brocanteurs (antique and junk dealers' fair) third weekend of
August all day at the place du Marché in the
center of this exquisite resort overlooking Lake
Geneva (Lac Léman). Information from the Office de Tourisme, rue des Bains, 01220 Divonne-
les-Bains, telephone 50.20.01.22, or the organizer, M. Dubois, 5 avenue de Genève, 74160
Saint-Julien-en-       Genevois,       telephone
50.49.27.40.

## Durtal 49430
(Please also see Angers.)

Grande rendez-vous de la brocante (grand junk
meet) last Sunday of September all day (beginning early, about 5:30 a.m.) in this town near
Angers. This is one of the largest once- a-year
markets in France, with over five hundred vendors mainly from surrounding regions, but
some from elsewhere. Many small items—including faience and pottery, vineyard equipment
and old bottles, as well as 19th-century furniture
and old gas lamps and chandeliers. Occasionally you'll find silver and arms. Information is
available from the organizers, Association An-
gevine    Arts    et    Traditions    Populaires
(A.A.A.T.P.), Mme. Bellec, La Jocolière, 123
Grand' Rue, 49140 Jarzé, telephone 41.89.42.65,
or M. Marc Roy, 5 rue Geoffroy l'Asnier, 75004
Paris, telephone 42.77.83.44.

**Eauze 32800**

Salon des Antiquaires (antique dealers' salon) for one week and two weekends during the first half of May. (Even after 16 years, they haven't gotten the dates consistent for every year!) The entire village center as serves the market place. Information from the M. Fourtou, Syndicat d'Initiative, place Mairie, 32800 Eauze, telephone 62.09.85.62.

**Ecouen 95440**

Petit marché aux puces (little flea market) third Sunday of every month at place de l'Eglise. This small market is close enough to Paris (less than 20 kilometers) to reflect Parisian prices and tastes.

**Enghien-les-Bains 95880**

Salle des Ventes (public sales hall) auctions usually twice a month (call for exact dates and times). This suburban town is only about 20 kilometers from Paris, and the items offered reflect Parisian taste and prices. You'll especially find 19th-century furniture. Information and sales at the Salle des Ventes, 2 rue du Docteur Leray, 95880 Enghien-les- Bains, telephone 34.12.68.16.

Foire d'antiquités et brocante (antique and junk fair) in mid January at the Salle des Fêtes. This is a reasonably large fair, which benefits in quality but not price from its proximity to Paris. Information from La Crémaillère, 19 rue de Chantilly, 50270 Gouvieux, telephone 44.56.11.60.

**Etampes 91150**

Salle des Ventes (public sales hall) auction every Sunday at 2 p.m. Inspection of merchandise and buyer registration takes place before the sale begins. Information and sales at the Salle des Ventes, place de Jeu de Paume, 91150 Etampes, telephone 64.94.02.33.

Salon des antiquaires (antique dealers' salon) in mid-September at the Salle des Fêtes on avenue Bonnevaux. This is a relatively minor show about 50 kilometers from Paris. Information from M. Locquet, La Libéronière, 8 carrefour des Religieuses, 91150 Etampes.

## Fayence 83440

Foire de la brocante (junk fair) first weekend of August (includes Friday, Saturday, and Sunday) at place de l'Eglise in the center of this Provençal village. Information from M. Allongue, Quartier du Lac-de-Tourettes, 83440 Fayence.

## Flaysoc 83780

Marché à la brocante (junk market) last Sunday of every month in the center of this small town in the hills of Provence near Draguignan. This relatively small but refreshing market, where you may see rustic Provençal items such as painted glassware, winegrowers' items, and occasional pieces of folk art. Information from the Office de Tourisme, 9 boulevard Clemenceau, 83300 Draguignan, telephone 94.68.63.30.

## Fontainebleau 77300

Salle des Ventes (public sales hall) auctions every Wednesday morning and Saturday and Sunday afternoon. The items here run more toward high finish and elegance than country rusticity. You may find bronze statues, cutglass chandeliers, and beautiful furniture of oak or fruitwood. Inspection of merchandise and buyer registration is held the afternoon before the Wednesday sales and in the morning before the weekend sales. Information and sales at the Salle des Ventes, 5 rue Royale—

place du Château, 77300 Fontainebleau,
telephone 64.22.27.62.

## Gerardmer 88400

Salon des antiquaires et brocanteurs (antique
and junk dealers' salon) first weekend of August
in and on the grounds of the Parc et Hôtel
Bragard. This is a large regional fair held in the
most elegant hotel in the area. Dozens of dealers
offer Lorraine's furniture (pine and hardwood),
crystal, and bric-a-brac. Information from the
Office de Tourisme, place Déportés, 88400,
telephone 29.63.08.74, or Grand Hotel Bragard,
place Tilleul, telephone 29.63.06.31, or the organizer, M. Dubois, 5 avenue de Genève, 74160
Saint-       Julien-en-Genevois,      telephone
50.49.27.40.

## Gien 45500

Foire des antiquités et brocante (antique and
junk fair) the fourth weekend (Saturday, Sunday, and Monday) of August on the Esplanade de
la Loire and Quai de Sully. This lively sale on
the south bank of the Loire (across the bridge
from the main part of Gien) draws about a
hundred vendors, with lots of items, including
old harnesses and tack, hunting items, provincial furniture, and chandeliers. Many but not all
vendors are dealers, mainly from the region. Information is available from the M. Germain,
A.C.A. de Gien, Mairie de Gien, 45500 Gien,
telephone 38.67.00.01.

## Granville 50400

Salle des Ventes (public sales hall) auction every
Saturday and Sunday year round at 2:30 p.m.
Inspection and buyer registration is held before
the auction begins. This market has specialties
of the region, including faience, domestic pottery, copper pots and pans, and occasionally
heavy provincial furniture, especially armoires
(often more than eight feet tall). Information and

sales at the Salle des Ventes, rue Jeanne Jugan, 50499 Granville, telephone 33.50.03.01.

## Grasse 06130

Marché à la brocante (junk market) every Wednesday morning year round at place Jean Jaurès in the center of the old city. This market is part of the regular food market and takes place around the public market hall. Street parking is almost impossible in this close-packed town; the only parking lots are near the Porte Neuve or place Martelli. In this home of the French perfume and flower industry, there are sometimes interesting items including Provençal folk art— and fewer tourists than along the nearby Riviera coast. Information from the Office de Tourisme, place Foux, 06130 Grasse, telephone 93.36.03.56, or M. Hans, 13 place Jean Jaurès, 06130 Grasse, telephone 73.36.36.25.

## Grenoble 38000

Marché à la brocante (junk market) third Monday of the month year round at place Saint-André in the old city center. This market seems to be where dealers buy and sell among themselves. Finds of regional items can be made here, but there's not much furniture. Information from the Office de Tourisme, rue République, 38000 Grenoble, telephone 76.54.34.36.

Marché aux puces du vieux Grenoble (flea market of old Grenoble) second Sunday of the month from March through June and October through December on rue Saint-Laurent, only a block form the river Isère in the old city center. The setting is picturesque, in one of the major provincial cities of France. Likely finds include cream pots and water jugs, butter molds, and occasional religious items. Information from the Office de Tourisme, rue République, 38000 Grenoble, telephone 76.54.34.36.

Salon Européen des antiquaires (European antique dealers' salon) every year for 10 days around the end of January and first week of February at the Alpexpo congress hall, about five kilometers south of the town center on avenue J. Perrot near the Village Olympique. Information from Alpexpo, Boîte Postale 788, 38034 Grenoble Cedex, telephone 76.09.80.26.

## Guerande 44350

Salon des antiquaires (antique dealers' salons) third week of July and the week in which Assumption Day falls (around August 15). This is a regional fair of about 50 dealers. Information from M. Boisguerin, Impasse de la Prévote, 44350 Guerande, telephone 40.24.93.87.

## Guingamp 22200

Foire à la brocante (junk fair) fourth weekend (including Friday) of October at the Hall des Foires et Expositions in this small Breton town. This is a minor regional fair. Information from Foire et Exposition, Boîte Postale 171, 22204 Guingamp Cedex.

## Haguenau 67500

Salon des antiquaires et brocanteurs (antique and junk dealers' salon) second weekend of September at the Hall du Manège. This provincial fair is often a good place to find Alsatian pottery and furniture. Information from the Office de Tourisme, Place J. Thierry, 67500 Haguenau, telephone 88.73.30.41, or from the organizer, M. Dubois, 5 avenue de Genève, 74160 Saint-Julien- en-Genevois, telephone 50.49.27.40.

## Hericourt 70400

Marché aux puces (flea market) third Sunday of every month year round. This relatively small market is of slight interest, though you may find old copper casseroles and faience.

## Havre

(Please see Le Havre)


## Hyères 83400

Marché aux puces (flea market) every Sunday
morning on avenue de la Pinade in the La Capte
district. This lively market in a Mediterranean
shore town near Toulon is part of the colorful
food and general merchandise market. Vendors
offer glassware (but not crystal), maritime items,
souvenirs, some folk art, and a few wood carvings. Information from Mairie de la Capte, 83400
Hyères, telephone 94.58.00.45.


## Isle-Adam

(Please see L'Isle-Adam.)


## Isle-sur-Sorgue

(Please see L'Isle-sur-Sorgue.)


## Joigny 89300

Salle des Ventes (public sales hall) auction every
Saturday or Sunday (it varies) at 2:30 p.m.
This picturesque Burgundian town often is a
good source of 19th-century furniture and occasional old tapestries. Inspection of merchandise and buyer registration is held the the day
before and morning of the sale. Information
and sales at the Salle des Ventes, 34 rue Aristide
Briand, 89300 Joigny, telephone 86.62.00.75.


## Lacroix-Saint-Ouen 60610

Hôtel des Ventes des Particuliers (public sales
hall) auctions irregularly during the year. Only
furniture and wood items are dealt with at this
auction. Information and sales conducted by Ser-

vice Conseil des Frères Nordin, at the Hôtel
des Ventes, 4 bis avenue de la Forêt, 60610
Lacroix-Saint-Ouen, telephone 44.41.56.88.

## Lamorlaye 60260

Exposition d'antiquaires (antique dealers' exposition) during October at the Salle des Fêtes.
This is is minor show with several dozen dealers,
held in this town not too far from Paris. Information from La Crémaillere, 19 rue de Chantilly,
50270 Gouvieux, telephone 44.56.11.60.

## Laon  02000

Salles des Ventes (public sales hall) auction
every Saturday at 2:30 p.m. year round. Inspection and buyer registration take place before the
sale begins. Information and sales at Salles des
Ventes, 1 rue Roze, 02000 Laon, telephone
23.23.47.27.

## La Rochelle 17000

Marché aux puces (flea market) every Saturday from April through September and the
first and third Saturday of months from October
through March on rue St. Nicolas. This is part of
the regular food and fish market; the setting is
picturesque and often more interesting than
the items and collectables offered. There is normal bric-a-brac, massive copper basins, and occasionally odds and ends from Asia and the
Caribbean. At one time, La Rochelle was the
main seaport of France, with a monopoly over
trade with France's colonies. Information from
the Office de Tourisme, 10 rue Fleuriau, 17000
La Rochelle, telephone 46.41.14.68.

## La Roche-sur-Foron 74800

Salon des antiquaires et brocanteurs (antique
and junk dealers' salon) first weekend of November at Palais de la Foire. This is a regional fair

near Geneva (Switzerland), where several dozen dealers show rustic furniture from Savoy and miscellaneous odds and ends. Information from the Office de Tourisme, Place Andrevetan, 78400 La Roche-sur-Foron, telephone 50.03. 36.68, or from the organizer, M. Dubois, 5 avenue de Genève, 74160 Saint-Julien-en-Genevois, telephone 50.49.27.40.

## La Sayne-sur-Mer 83500

Marché à la brocante (junk market) first and third Wednesday of every month at Aux Sablettes. This market is a typical colorful Provençal market, with both tourist souvenirs and assorted normal flea market items. Information from the Office de Tourisme, 6 rue Léon Blum, 83500 La Seyne-sur- Mer, telephone 94.94.73.09.

## Le Havre 76600

Marché aux puces (flea market) every Thursday year round at the Place du Forum. This rather large market has numerous vendors of bibelots such as faience, glass, painted glass (a regional specialty), and cider cups. Information from the Office de Tourisme, Place Hôtel de Ville, 76600 Le Havre, telephone 35.42.39.32.

## Le Luc 83340

Marché à la brocante (junk market) every Saturday morning at Aux Liébords. This market in Provence has some interesting items such as glass (not crystal) and, sometimes, folk art. Information from the Office de Tourisme, Place Verdun, 83340 Le Luc, telephone 94.60.74.51 (open only from June 1 through August 31), or from the organizer, M. Bouillet, 7 bis rue de Mereu, 83340 Le Luc.

## Le Mans 72000

Marché aux puces (flea market) every Saturday morning on avenue de Paderborn at the foot of Cathedral, along the tree-shaded gardens. Information from the Office de Tourisme, 38 Place République, 72000 Le Mans, telephone 43.28.17.22.

24 heures de la brocante (24 hours of junk) the usually the second weekend of April (including Friday) throughout the old town above the river and near the cathedral. This is a major regional fair and worth the visit. Information from Prom'Art, 4 rue Offenbach, 35100 Rennes, telephone 99.50.74.19.

## Le Puy 43000

Petit marché aux puces (small flea market) Saturday morning from just before 8 a.m. to noon at the Place de Clauzel as part of the regular food market. There are usually only about a dozen vendors of antiques and junk. Le Puy is in a relatively poor part of France, but is one of the most beautiful of French towns in part because of the spiny heights that tower several hundred feet above the surrounding plains. Information from the Office de Tourisme, place du Breuil (only a couple of hundred meters from the market), 43000 Le Puy, telephone 71.09.27.42.

Salle des Ventes (public sales hall) auction every Thursday, every Monday, and the 15th day of every month at 2 p.m. Inspection of merchandise and buyer registration takes place before the sale. Information and sales at the Salle des Ventes, 10 boulevard de la République, 43000 Le Puy, telephone 71.09.03.85.

## Les Sables d'Olonne 85100

Marché aux puces (flea market) first Sunday of the month year round at Place de la Chaume. This Atlantic seaside summer resort's market is nothing special; you may find vendors offering marine items, local pottery, and small agricultural tools. Information from the Office de Tourisme, rue Maréchal Leclerc, 85100 Les Sables d'Olonne, telephone 51.32.03.28.

## Lille 59000

Lille and its surrounding area are hardly tourist country; full of slag heaps, grimy brick buildings, and steel mills. However, it is full of promise for the antique collector and dealer, because it is the center of France's decaying and economically depressed Rust Belt.

(Please also see Roubaix.)

Marché de Wazemmes (Wazemmes market) Sunday morning year round from dawn to about noon around the Parvis de Croix and Place de la Nouvelle Aventure and surrounding the Eglise Saint-Pierre (church). The general market, with food, clothes, and miscellaneous items, occupies a paved lot and a 19th-century cast-iron market hall, but the flea market is off to the east side. About a 120 dealers and private parties sell all kinds of items, including silver and silver plate, brass, crystal chandeliers, bottles and glass, old signs, and lots of 19th- century furniture, including chairs, chests of drawers, and hope chests. This is one of the best flea markets in France: prices are reasonable and quality is relatively high.

    Parking is available on the street, but is difficult to find after 8 a.m. Access by public transit to the Gambetta station, then walk to the church, visible over one row of houses. Information from the Office de Tourisme, Palais Rihour, Place Rihour, 59000 Lille, telephone 20.55.29.44. A branch tourist office office is found at the main railroad station.

Marché aux puces (flea market) Saturday afternoon at rue de la Monnaie and Place du Concert. This market, smaller than the Sunday Marché de Wazemmes, is still worth attending and offers similar items. Information from the Office de Tourisme, Palais Rihour, Place Rihour, 59000 Lille, telephone 20.55.29.44.

Bienniale de l'antiquité et de la brocante (anti-que and brocante biennial show) second weekend of odd- numbered years at the Foire Internation-ale de Lille, near the main railway station. This is one of the major provincial shows in France, and is well worth attending. Access by car is from the avenue Julien Destrée exit from the ring road. The nearest subway station is Gares, at the railway station; then walk several hundred meters. Organized by the Foire Internationale de Lille, 59000 Lille, telephone 20.52.79.60.

## Limoges 87000

Petit marché aux puces (little flea market) every Wednesday and Saturday from early morning until about 12:30 p.m. at the tree-shaded Place d'Aine (facing the Palais de Justice), a block away from the food and general market. You'll often find minor pieces of Limoges porcelain, but most will be of medium to low quality. You also may find farm implements, andirons, pokers, and shovels. Information from the Office de Tourisme, Boulevard Fleurus, 87000 Limoges, telephone 55.34.46.87.

Salon des antiquaires (antique dealers' salon) first and second weekends of June. This is a major regional show with around 100 vendors, all of whom are full-time dealers. You'll find massive farm furniture, as well as porcelain and pottery. Information from the Office de Tourisme, Boulevard Fleurus, 87000 Limoges, telephone 55.34.46.87, or from the organizers, Prom'Art, 4 rue Offenbach, telephone 99.50. 74.19.

## L'Isle-Adam 95290

Petit marché aux puces (little flea market) third Sunday of every month in this small town in Paris' outskirts. Because of its proximity to Paris, prices are as high as in Paris and selec-tion is similar though much smaller. Information

from the Office de Tourisme, 1 avenue de
Paris, 95290 L'Isle-Adam, telephone 34.69.09.76.

## L'Isle-sur-la-Sorgue 84800

This small town in Provence, near Avignon and
Cavaillon, promotes itself as an antiques center. There are frequent large markets and
fairs, some of the best in the region.

Marché aux puces et isle de la brocante (flea
market and junk island), two markets that face
each other across the water in the village center.
The junk market takes place all day Saturday
and Sunday, and can attract over 100 vendors on
some days. The flea market, also on the water,
takes place all day Sunday, though it quiets
down around lunch time. These markets are
often places to find Provençal antiques, such as
carved olive wood, pottery, glassware, and, rarely, Santons dolls. Information from M. Albert
Gassier, Boîte Postale 45, 84800 L'Isle-sur-la-
Sorgue, telephone 90.38.10.43.

Foire à la brocante (junk fair) twice a year:
Easter Week and the Easter Monday (the day
after Easter), and the Assumption Day
weekend (second Thursday through following
Monday of August). This fair is a much larger
version of the regular markets and, especially in
August, attracts thousands of visitors. Information from M. Albert Gassier, Boîte Postale 45,
84800 L'Isle-sur-la-Sorgue, telephone 90.38.
10.43.

Village d'Antiquaires et Brocanteurs (antique
and junk dealers' village) open Saturday, Sunday, and Monday year round at Village d'Antiquaires et Brocanteurs next to the railway station. This building is home to about 40 dealers,
who offer large quantities of Provençal furniture,
folk items such as glassware, farm tools, and
copper cauldrons, and just plain junk, but no
readily apparent reproductions. For information call 90.38.04.57.

## Luxieul-les-Bains 70300

Grande foire aux antiquaires et brocanteurs
(grand antique and junk dealers' fair) the last
weekend of August at Place du 8-Mai. This is a
regional fair in spite of the grand name—and
is refreshing. Likely finds could include
glassware, faience, and rustic wooden items. Information from the Office de Tourisme, 1 rue
Thermes, telephone 84.40.06.41, or the organizer, M. Dubois, 5 avenue de Genève, 74160
Saint-Julien-en- Genevois, telephone 50.49.
27.40.

## Lyon 69000

The ancient city of Lyon dates from before the
days of the Romans; Roman ruins can be seen.
For centuries Lyon has been rich: a major
crossroads and center of the cloth trade, and
an early center of printing. It is also widely acknowledged to be the home of the best of French
cuisine.

Marché aux puces de la Beyssine (flea market at
Beyssine) Thursday, Saturday, and especially
Sunday morning year round from early morning to about 1 p.m. at 1 bis rue Joseph Merlin in
the northeastern suburb of Vulx-en-Velin,
upstream along the along the Rhone canal.
This grubby market is by far the largest in Lyon.
Hundreds of (mostly Arab) vendors push piles of
used clothing, car parts, bike parts, and used
cars as you approach the octagonal building in
the center of the large dusty (or muddy) field.
    The building in the center is where about
170 dealers offer a jumble of small antiques
and lots of junk in the permanent stalls and
tables rented by the day in the octagon's open-air
center. While there are thousands of items,
including glass, silver, porcelain, massive
furniture, and ironwork, this is one market
where you need to know exactly what you're
looking at. There are no warranties or
guarantees given at this market. Toilets are
available in the building, are filthy, and cost 1
franc.

Parking is difficult and frustrating; only distant street parking is available, since only sellers can park on the grounds. Park where you can and follow the crowds. Access by public transit on the Metro to the Bonneray station, then walk along the canal, and cross the first bridge you come to, following the crowds, or take busses 51, 56, or 57 to the corner of the Pont de Plaisance and rue Balland, and then walk. Information from Association Brocante Feyssine, 17-19 rue Rouget-de-l'Isle, 69100 Villeurbanne, telephone 78.93.40.19 for information or 78.93.44.37 for the market commissioner.

Brocante Stalingrad (Stalingrad junk market) Thursday and Saturday from about 8:30 a.m. until noon and 2 p.m. to 6 p.m., and Sunday from 9 a.m. to 1 p.m. at 113-115 Boulevard Stalingrad, across the railroad tracks from the Parc de la Tête d'Or. The name "brocante" belies the place: in actuality it is an antique dealers' center, containing approximately 200 dealers of medium to high quality items. A few items are of museum quality (and priced accordingly, though less than usual in Paris). You'll find massive furniture from the 17th through early 20th centuries, porcelain and crystal in abundance, massive silver flatware and quantities of silver plate, paintings (mainly from the 19th-century), bronzes, and a few old books. These items are often refined rather than country-style primitives. Thursdays are peaceful; this is the day the antique trade comes. Weekends are crowded, boisterous, and it takes far longer to see what there is.

Parking is easy on Thursday on Boulevard Stalingrad directly across from the market between the street and the railroad embankment. On weekends, either arrive very early or plan to walk quite a way. Access by Metro or train to the Brotteaux station, then follow the tracks north for about 500 meters. Information from Brocante Stalingrad, 113-115 Boulevard Stalingrad, 69100 Villeurbanne, telephone 78.89.30.68 or 78.93.91.25.

Marché permanent d'antiquités (permanent antique dealers' market) open weekdays from

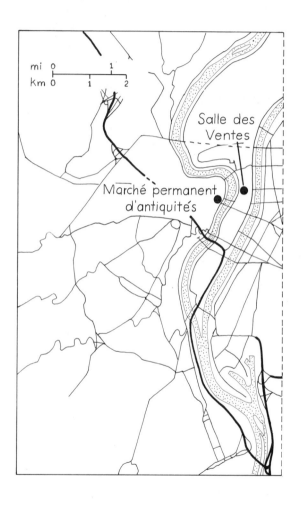

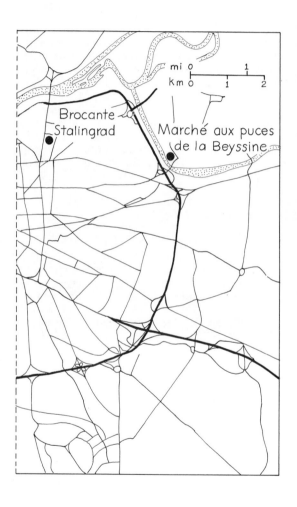

about 9 to 12 a.m. and 3 to 6 p.m. on Quai Romain-Rolland along the west bank of the Saône river in the old medieval section of Lyon. Several dozen dealers offer good-quality items at relatively high prices. Access by Metro to the Cordeliers station, then 300 walk meters west and across the river to the Quai Romain-Rolland. Parking is available in lots between the Quai and the river, though on weekdays the lots are often crowded. Street parking is hard to find.

Salle des Ventes (public sales hall) auction every Monday and Wednesday at 2 p.m. Viewing and buyer registration is accomplished in the morning before the sale. Information and sales at the Salle des Ventes, 31 rue des Tuiliers, 69000 Lyon, telephone 78.00.86.65.

## Mâcon 71000

Salle des Ventes (public sales hall) auction every Saturday at 2:30 p.m. You're likely to find fine old walnut Burgundian furniture and chairs at this sale. Buyer registration and inspection of merchandise takes place the day before and on the morning of the sale. Information and sales at the Salle des Ventes, 1054 Quai de Lattre-de-Tassigny, 71000 Mâcon, telephone 85.38.75.07.

Foire à la brocante (junk fair) the first weekend of December at the Palais de la Foire along the river on the north side of the town. This is a relatively small regional fair. Information from Promonet, 401 rue de Fontenailles, 71000 Mâcon.

## Magny-en-Vexin 95000

Salon d'antiquités et brocante (antique and junk salon) in mid-June (varies from year to year) at the Salle des Fêtes. This is a small fair not too far from Paris. Information from La Cremaillère, 19 rue de Chantilly, 60270 Gouvieux, telephone 44.56.11.60.

## Maisons-Laffitte 78600

Exposition d'antiquaires (antique show) at the Chateau in September (contact the organizer for exact dates). Organized by La Cremaillère, 19 rue de Chantilly, 60270 Gouvieux, telephone 44.56.11.60.

## Mantes-la-Jolie 78200

Foire de brocante (junk fair) last weekend of June at Centre Commercial Val Fourré. This minor fair is held in the Val Fourre shopping center. Organized by SADEMA, 17 rue Saint-Paul, 75004 Paris, telephone 48.87.58.48.

## Marseille 13000

(Please also see Aubagne.)

Salle des Ventes (public sales hall) auctions every Wednesday, Friday, and Saturday at 2:30 p.m. at 19 rue Borde. Public inspection and registration is held before the sale. Information from the Salle des Ventes, 19 rue Borde, 13000 Marseille, telephone 91.79.46.30.

Salon des antiquaires (antique dealers' salon) third week of October from 10 a.m. to 7 p.m. at the Parc Chanot convention hall on the southern side of Marseille along Boulevards Rabatau and Michelet. This is one of the major regional shows in southern France, with an emphasis on jewelry. Organized by M. Grobon Ghiglione, S.A.F.I.M. Parc Chanot, 13266 Marseille Cedex 2, telephone 91.76.16.00.

Quartier de cours Julien (Julien Court arcade) antique row, a tree-shaded street home to about 30 permanent dealers. The second Sunday of the month, the shops spill out into the street, especially in the morning. This street is just off the cours Lieutand not far from La Canebière, the colorful boulevard that is the heart of Marseille. Information from cours Julien, telephone 91.42.79.35.

## Meaux 77100

Marché aux puces (flea market) last Sunday of every month in the town center. This is not a major market, since it is too close to Paris (about 50 kilometers). Information from the Office de Tourisme, 2 rue Notre-Dame, 77100 Meaux, telephone 64.33.02.26.

Salle des Ventes (public sales hall) auction every Saturday and Sunday at 2 p.m. The proximity to Paris tends to bring out more highly polished items than country pieces. You'll find furniture, crystal, some porcelains, mostly from the 19th century. Inspection of items and buyer registration is held in the morning before the sale. Information and sales at the Salle des Ventes, 54 rue de l'Abreuvoir, 77100 Meaux, telephone 64.34.11.97.

## Menton 06500

Marché aux puces (flea market) every Friday year round as part of the public market on Quai de Monleón. Parking is available in a lot across the street. This small market draws fewer tourists than those of Nice or Cannes. Information from the Office de Tourisme, at the Palais de l'Europe on avenue Boyer, 06500 Menton, telephone 93.35.77.39.

## Meounes 83136

Marché aux puces (flea market) every Saturday (including a general market) and Marché à la brocante (junk market) every Monday morning (early!) on Boulevard Jean-Jaurès. These markets in this village near Toulon in Mediterranean Provence are well worth a visit to find rustic junk, including rustic glass, small pieces of furniture, minor jewelry, as well as normal bric-a-brac and bibelots.

**Metz 57000**

Marché aux puces (flea market) first and third Saturday of every month year round at the grounds of the Foire Internationale in the suburban Griay district. Here you'll find about 100 vendors; among the junk you may find crystal (especially Saint-Louis, which is manufactured locally), faience, and heavy copperware. Information from the Office de Tourisme, Porte de Serpenois, 57000 Metz, telephone 87.75.65.21.

Salon des antiquaires (antique dealers' salon) for about a week the fourth weekend of November. You may find beautiful rustic pine furniture and exquisite fruitwood marquetry furniture at this fair, as well as quantities of crystal, silver, and silver plate. This is a major regional fair, and is well worth attending. Organized by M. Vayssade, F. I. M., Salon des Antiquaires, Boîte Postale 5059, 57072 Metz Cedex, telephone 87.75.49.55.

**Meyrargues 13650**

Foire des brocanteurs (junk dealers' fair) the end of May and beginning of June (varies from year to year) throughout this small town. This major regional fair, near Aix- en-Provence, has almost 100 vendors (mostly dealers) with all kinds of bibelots, folk art, faience, and other odds and ends. Information from the organizer, M. Claude Giraud, telephone 42.57.50.57.

**Mirande 32300**

Salon des antiquaires (antique dealers' salon) the weekend surrounding and also including Bastille Day (July 14) throughout the village center. This is a regional show, but discoveries of rustic items and country furniture sometimes can make it worthwhile. The date makes it a festive and entertaining (as well as heavily attended) show. Information from the Syndicat d'Initiative, 9 rue Victor Hugo, 32300 Mirande, telephone 62.66.68.10.

## Montauban 82000

Marché aux puces (flea market) every Saturday morning (early!) at Place Prax-Paris, in the
town center. This market is part of the food
and general merchandise market. Because this
part of central France has never been very
rich, you're likelier to find domestic and rustic
farm items such as copper basins, fired clay jugs
and casseroles, and some folk art than
polished, stylish decorative pieces. Since traditional furniture of the region consists of heavy
and massive pieces, you won't often find much of
it at this market. Information from the Office de
Tourisme, rue Collége Montauban, 82000 Montauban, telephone 63.63.60.60.

Salon des antiquaires et brocanteurs de Quercy
(Quercy regional antique and junk dealers'
salon) first Thursday through following Sunday
of December at the Salle des Fêtes de Montauban. This fair is a good place to find
regional furniture (measure the height before
buying!) as well as small items of the region. Expert appraisers are on duty. Organized by
GERM, 82000 Montauban, telephone
63.63.00.40.

## Mont-de-Marsan 40000

Marché aux puces (flea market) first Wednesday
of every month year round at. the Place des
Arènes, across the street from the railway station. This is a relatively small country-style
market, worth seeing if you're in the area but
not worth a special journey. Street parking is
available at the railway station. Information
from the Office de Tourisme, 22 rue Victor Hugo,
40000 Mont-de-Marsan, telephone 58.75.38.67.

## Montferrand 63100

(Please see Clermont-Ferrand.)

## Montluçon 03100

Marché à la brocante (junk market) third Sunday of the month year round. Information from the Office de Tourisme, 1 ter avenue Marx-Dormoy, 03100 Montluçon, telephone 70.06.71.15.

## Montpellier 34000

Marché aux puces (flea market) Saturday morning (beginning at dawn) every Saturday year round at the place des Arceaux, about 1 kilometer west of the city center, near the west end of the Aqueduc Saint-Clement, which begins at Promenade Peyrou. This is one of the best markets in France and offers lots of old objects seemingly from the wine trade in addition the the usual flea market bric-a-brac. You'll also find books—probably since the city is the home of an ancient university. Information from the Office de Tourisme, Place Comédie, 34000 Montpellier, telephone 87.60.76.90. A branch tourist office is at the Gare S.N.C.F. (main rail station).

Salon des antiquaires et de la brocante (antique and junk dealers' salon) beginning about the 25th of April and continuing through the second Sunday of May at the Parc des Expositions in the Montpellier-Fréjorgues district. The two days before the show is opened to the public are reserved for dealer sales—bring your business card and maybe a copy of your business license. This is the preeminent show of the region; about two hundred dealers bring small art, including bronzes, glass, local books, and engravings. Large quantities of furniture and local arts are also for sale. Access is easy by car; parking is available at the site. Organized by F. I. V. V. de Montpellier, Boîte Postale 1056, 34006 Montpellier Cedex, telephone 67.64.12.12.

## Montreuil-sur-Mer 62170

Salle des Ventes (public sales hall) auction every Saturday and the last Sunday of every month at

3 p.m. Inspection and buyer registration is held before the sale begins. Information and sale at the Salle des Ventes, 29 Grand rue, 62170 Montreuil-sur-Mer, telephone 21.06.05.70.

## Mouans-Sartoux 06370

Foire à la brocante (junk fair) third weekend of July (Saturday, Sunday, and Monday) all day every year at the square de la Poste. This Provençal village is just 10 kilometers from Cannes, on the Riviera. This is a major fair and is well worth attending if you're in the area. Organized by the Syndicat d'Initiative, telephone 93.75.51.99.

Salon des antiquaires et brocanteurs (antique and junk dealers' salon) in mid-April at Place de l'Eglise. This fair is of local importance. Information from the Syndicat d'Initiative, telephone 93.75.51.99.

## Nancy 54000

Marché aux puces (flea market) second Saturday of the month year round on the Grande Rue in the Old Town in the city center. This market, set among ancient overhanging buildings, is also one of the best markets in France. Lorraine is one of France's economically declining industrial areas, always a good sign when looking for antiques and collectables. Specialties of the region you may find include crystal by Baccarat and Daum, wood carvings and religious statues, chimney plaques, and faience.

While you're at the market, see the place Stanislaus only a block away, which is one of the most beautiful ensembles of 18th- century civic architecture in the world.

Information from the Office de Tourisme, 14 Place Stanislaus, 54000 Nancy, telephone 83.35.03.01. Organized by Mme. Quill', Boutique Bergamote, 10 rue Saint-Epure, 54000 Nancy, telephone 83.36.56.68.

Salon des antiquités et de la brocante (antique and junk salon) during mid-April (check, because exact dates vary each year) at the Parc des Expositions, about 2 kilometers south of the city center where boulevard Berthout turns into the autoroute. A major regional fair of around 100 dealers; lots of parking is available on the site. Organized by M. Detourbet, Salon des Antiquités, Boîte Postale 1593, 54027 Nancy Cedex, telephone 83.51.09.01.

## Nantes 44000

Marché aux puces, Saturday morning (early!) year round at place Viarme. The first weekend of October, this becomes one of the major markets of the fall season. This large irregular square is about one kilometer north west of the Chateau and about two hundred meters west the main food and general market on rue Talensac. This market is one of the better and larger flea markets in France, where you may find Chinese porcelain, Delftware, and local faience and domestic pottery, and "LU" biscuit tins. Since Nantes is one of the major seaports of France, this market sometimes has quantities of foreign antiques (especially from England). Information from the Office de Tourisme, Place Change, 44000 Nantes, telephone 40.47.04.51.

Salles des Ventes (public auction halls) auctions every Monday, Wednesday, and Friday at 2 p.m. This is one of the major provincial auctions—well worth attending. Local specialties include furniture and maritime items. Inspection and buyer registration takes place during regular business hours and before the sale begins. Information and sale at Salles des Ventes, 55 rue Léon Jost, 44000 Nantes, telephone 40.59.13.13.


## Narbonne 11100

Marché aux puces (flea market) Thursday morning year round at place Voltaire. This small but interesting market specializes in folk art, local paintings, glass, and sometimes winegrowing equipment. At the beginning of July, the fair is extended through the weekend and is much larger and more interesting, with hundreds of buyers. Organized by the Service des Marchés, Ville de Narbonne, 11100 Narbonne, telephone 68.32.31.60. Information is also available from the Office de Tourisme, Place J. Salengro, 11100 Narbonne, telephone 68.65.15.60.


## Nevers 58000

Foire à la brocante (junk fair) second half of April at the Maison des Sports et de la Culture. This is a regional show in a relatively untouristed city in central France. Organized by Prom'Art, 4 rue Offenbach, 35100 Rennes, telephone 99.50.74.19.


## Nice 06000

Marché de la brocante, livres, et friperie (junk, book, and used clothes market) every day except Sunday from 8 a.m. to 1 p. m. and 3 p.m. to 5 p.m. at Boulevard Risso and the adjoining Quai du Paillon. This market consists of about 80 permanent vendors installed in sheds, selling all kinds of junk. Selection is acceptable but not grand; skilled and informed vendors make true finds rare, though the atmosphere is interesting.

Parking is available on the street (though difficult to find) or underground under the central median of the boulevard. Organized by the Ville de Nice, Service des Marchés, Hôtel de Ville, 06000 Nice, telephone 93.82.16.30.

Marché aux puces (flea market) every Monday year round on cours Saleya, in the old central city. This is part of the colorful general merchandise, flower, and food market. Though you'll probably not make any great finds, you could find some Italian work, or neglected silver plate. Organized by the Ville de Nice, Service des Marchés, Hôtel de Ville, 06000 Nice, telephone 93.82.16.30.

La Promenade des Antiquaires (antique dealers' gallery) open every day except Wednesday at 7 Promenade des Anglais, is a gathering of about two dozen dealers offering quality coupled with relatively high prices. A pay parking garage is available nearby on the rue Massena.

## Nîmes 30000

Petit marché aux puces (little flea market) every Monday year round on the Allée Jean-Jaurès near place J. Guesde. This market is on a rather gritty and dusty boulevard, and is also the location of a produce market. Quality is poor, but if you look, you might find something. Free street parking is ample, though toilets are nonexistent.

Do not confuse this market with the food market hall on the rue du Planas in the city center, which has one of the finest food markets in France. Information from the Office de Tourisme, 6 rue Auguste, 30000 Nîmes, telephone 66.67.28.10. Organized by Ville de Nîmes, Bureau Numéro 13, L'attaché du Service des Foires et Marchés, Hôtel de Ville, 30000 Nîmes, telephone 66.76.70.01.

Petit marché aux puces (little flea market) Sunday morning year round at the place des Carmes. This is a smaller market than the Monday market, but there are antiques and the quality tends to be better. Information from the Office de Tourisme, 6 rue Auguste, 30000 Nîmes, telephone 66.67.28.10. Organized by Ville de Nîmes, Bureau Numéro 13, L'attaché du

Service des Foires et Marchés, Hôtel de Ville, 3000 Nîmes, telephone 66.76.70.01.

Salon des Antiquaires et Brocanteurs (antique and junk dealers' salon) the entire second week of December at the Parc des Expositions on rue de Bouillargues, on the eastern edge of the city. Take rue de Bouillarges under the railway tracks from Boulevard Talabot, the main street along the tracks; the Parc des Expositions is about 200 meters past the tunnel. There is also the Journées Nationales de la Brocante (National Junk Days) at the same place at the beginning of March. Information from M. Verdelhan, Salon des Antiquaires, Parc des Expositions, rue de Bouillargues, 30000 Nîmes, telephone 66.84.93.39.

## Niort 79000

Petit marché à la brocante (little flea market) first Wednesday of every month year round in the market hall in the center of town along the river. This provincial town in central France offers only occasional finds. Information from the Office de Tourisme, place Poste, 79000 Niort, telephone 49.24.18.79.

## Nogent-le-Rotrou 28400

Salle des Ventes (public auction hall) auctions every Saturday year round at 2 p.m. and every Sunday from 10 a.m. to 2 p.m. Inspection of merchandise and buyer registration is held before the sale. Information and sales at the Salle des Ventes, 13 rue Abbé-Beule, 28400 Nogent-le-Rotrou, telephone 37.52.01.85.

## Obernai 67210

Foire à la brocante (junk fair) twice a year: the second Wednesday through Sunday of May and October 31 through November 2, at the Salle des Fêtes. Obernai is a picturesque town in Alsace; at the fair you'll find massive country furniture, blue pottery wine pitchers, and stoneware crocks, among other items. Information from M. Kleim, 21 place de l'Etoile, 67210 Obernai, telephone 88.95.52.80.

## Orange 84100

Marché aux puces (flea market) every Friday morning at the Place des Cordeliers. This market, which has only a few dealers in antiques and junk, is mainly a food and general merchandise market. Information from the Office de Tourisme, 6 cours Aristide Briand, 84100 Orange, telephone 90.51.80.06.

Salon des antiquaires (antique dealers' salon) the last Friday of May through the second following Sunday at the Palais de la Foire in the Parc des Expositions. This regional fair is organized by C.O.S.A.P.O., 4 rue Gabriel-Boissy, 84100 Orange.

## Orléans 45000

Marché aux puces (flea market) Saturday morning from about 7:30 a.m. on Boulevard Andre-Martin, the wide boulevard near the railway station. This boulevard is on the site of the now-demolished city walls. This market is part of the regular food and general merchandise market, and is worthwhile if you are in the area.

Street parking is available but difficult after about 8:30. There are underground pay parking garages directly under the marketplace. Information from the Office de Tourisme, Place Albert 1er., 45000 Orléans, telephone 38.53.05.95.

Galerie des Ventes (public sales gallery) auctions on variable dates during the year, but mostly in February and March, May and June, and November and December. The gallery is near the railroad bridge over the Loire on the east side of the city. A list of dates and times is available form the organizer, and a catalogue is available before each sale. Dates and sales times are also advertised in the Les Ventes Prochaines section of Gazette de l'Hôtel Drouot. These sales offer fine-quality antiques, particularly furniture. The sales take place and information is available from Galerie des Ventes, Mme. Sarot, boulevard Motte-Sanguin (Impasse Notre-Dame de Chemin), 45000 Orléans, telephone 38.62.67.84.

Foire aux antiquités et à la paperasse (antique and old papers fair) second week of March at the Parc des Expositions, rue du Robert Schumann, about 2 kilometers south of the Loire on way to the Parc Floral (follow the signs). An admission charge is made. This is a major regional fair. Information from the Parc des Expositions, Boîte Postale 5002, 45020 Orléans Cedex, telephone 38.66.28.20.

Salon d'Automne des antiquaires (autumn antique dealers' salon) for 10 days at the end of September and beginning of October at the Parc des Expositions, rue du Robert Schumann, about 2 kilometers south of the Loire on way to the Parc Floral (follow the signs). An admission charge is made. Information from the Parc des Expositions, Boîte Postale 5002, 45020 Orléans Cedex, telephone 38.66.28.20.

**Paris 75000**

(Please also see also Chatou, Corbielle-Essones, Etampes, Savigny-sur-Orge and Versailles.)

Paris is the undisputed center of the French antique trade, just as it is the undisputed center of France in things ranging from government and finance to books and retailing. Few other countries in the world are as centralized as France. Few other cities of the world are as rich in antiques, flea markets, and auctions as Paris (except London).

The flea market may have originated in Paris, in part as the result of the 19th century redesign of the city of Paris. This redesign forced the junk dealers and rag pickers to move outside the city gates. Once at the city gates of Paris, they stayed: even today the flea markets of Paris are at or near the city limits, conveniently (for motorists) near to the boulevard Périphérique ring expressway around Paris.

Weekends are when most flea markets in Paris are open, though there are antiques to be found every day of the week.

## Antique Shops

There are hundreds if not thousands of antique and junk shops in Paris; there are pages of them in the telephone book (look under "Antiquités"). Most shops seem to be centered in several districts: the Left Bank, near Saint-Germain- des-Pres, along rue Saint-Honoré, and near the Hôtel Drouot. Walk along the streets of any of these neighborhoods: you'll be attracted to antique shops as delectable as candy stores to children of all ages.

## Paris Flea Markets

Porte de Clignancourt—Saint-Ouen, Saturday, Sunday and Monday from dawn to about an hour before dusk. Early Saturday morning is the best time to find the new items; Monday afternoon is the best time to bargain with the dealers.

Clignancourt is the original, prototypical flea market, which has been in existence for much more than a century. In this period, it has grown from small to large to gigantic: it may be the largest single concentration of junk and antiques for sale in the world.

It is actually formed of six independently owned markets (Paul Bert, Biron, Cambo, Serpette, Jules Vallès, and Vernaison) within a few blocks of each other. Each has a different atmosphere and different specialties, but since they're all in the same neighborhood, they can be treated together. Each has between 80 and 300 stall holders (about 1200 in all) who open up late in the morning, from about 9:30 to as late as 11:30 a.m.

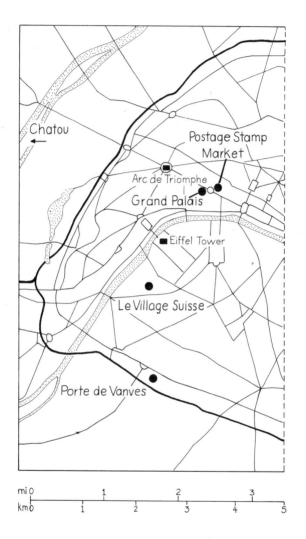

Chatou

Postage Stamp
Market

Arc de Triomphe

Grand Palais

■ Eiffel Tower

Le Village Suisse

Porte de Vanves

mi 0        1        2        3
km 0    1    2    3    4    5

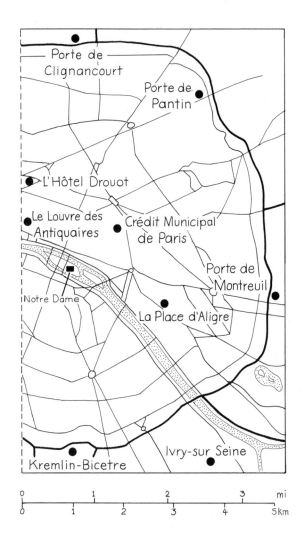

Porte de Clignancourt

Porte de Pantin

L'Hôtel Drouot

Le Louvre des Antiquaires

Crédit Municipal de Paris

Porte de Montreuil

Notre Dame

La Place d'Aligre

Kremlin-Bicetre

Ivry-sur Seine

| 0 | | 1 | | 2 | | 3 | mi |

| 0 | 1 | 2 | 3 | 4 | 5 km |

Probably 100 independent street merchants work out of suitcases, card tables, and cardboard boxes. They arrive early and usually are gone by 10:30, which is when the permanent booth holders in the established markets are just arriving and opening.

Remember as you work the alleys that all of these dealers are professionals and usually know the value of the merchandise. Though finds can occasionally be made, don't expect a long-lost painting by Watteau or Fragonard.

Parking is difficult on market day after about 7:30; there is street parking on the rue René Binet and surrounding streets. A pay parking garage is at the corner of avenue de la Porte de Clignancourt and rue de F. Croisset, but will often be full after about 9:30 in the morning.

Access by Metro to the Porte de Clignancourt station (end of the line) and walk under the underpass. The market is centered on the rue des Rosiers, the first diagonal street on your left, just past the underpass. You can also take bus 56 to the boulevard Périphérique.

Porte de Vanves, Saturday and Sunday from dawn to 5 p.m. on the school side of avenue Marc Sangnier and on avenue Georges Lafenestre between avenue Marc Sangnier to the bridge over the boulevard Périphérique. The market is on the southern edge of Paris, best before about 10 a.m. Furniture tends to be found on avenue Marc Sangnier; everything else is found throughout the market.

This market seems to be where Parisians go; you'll find all kinds of items of good quality, and reasonable prices. About 200 vendors, some full-time professionals and some apparently part- time collectors sell at this market. Some dealers from the Clignancourt market make their purchases here, then double the price for the tourists.

When it is not raining, you'll often see lots of massive pieces of furniture. On any day you'll find silver, silver plate, books, and crystal and glass. There are few clothes, and no food. No public toilets are to be found.

The market takes place in the street on avenue Georges Lafenestre and on the sidewalk along avenue Marc Sangier. There are no permanent vendors.

Street parking can be found on the street, but may require early arrival or a frantic search. There are no garages closer than the pay parking lot along the railroad tracks on the other side of the boulevard Périphérique.

Access by Metro to Porte de Vanves, then walk a short block south (toward the Pèriphèrique, which is underground) to avenue Marc Sangnier. You should see the vendors about halfway down the block.

Porte de Montreuil, Sunday morning from about 7 a.m. until just after noon. Access by Metro to the Porte de Montreuil station, then continue out (east) from the subway exit across the boulevard Périphérique. Just past the circle, you'll see the market on your left sandwiched between the expressway and the avenue du Professeur André Lemierre.

About 200 vendors of new and used clothes, kitchen gadgets, and lots of bric-a-brac cram into tiny space. About a third of the vendors sell used items, little furniture but lots of broken items and anonymous junk. This is a lower-class neighborhood (many blacks and especially Arabs), and the merchandise reflects the neighborhood's poverty.

Parking is available on surrounding streets, though you'll have to look. There are no parking garages in the neighborhood.

La Place d'Aligre, Tuesday through Sunday (especially on Sunday) from early morning to about 1 p.m. This market is hard to find, hidden away in the run-down eastern 12th Arrondisement.

This market has an abundance of cheap new and used clothes, food and vegetables, and about 20 to 40 dealers of brocante, bric-a- brac, and some battered furniture. While the choice is not as great as some other markets, prices are probably the lowest in Paris.

Parking is available on the street, but you will have to search for a space.

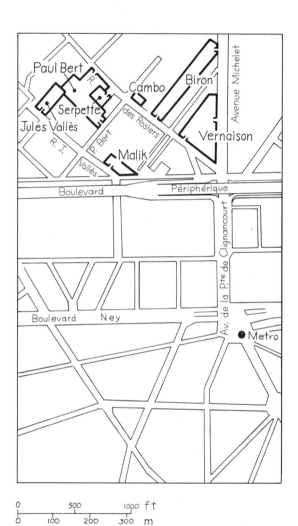

Paul Bert

R.

Cambo

Biron

Avenue Michelet

Serpette

des Rosiers

Jules Vallès

R. J.

P. Bert

Vernaison

Vallès

Malik

Boulevard

Périphérique

Av. de la Pte de Clignancourt

Boulevard Ney

● Metro

| 0 | | 500 | | 1000 ft |
| 0 | 100 | 200 | 300 | m |

Access by Metro to the Ledru-Rollin station, then walk east four blocks along rue du Faubourg Saint-Antoine to avenue d'Aligre. Turn right and at the end of the second block you'll see the market hall on your left (food and drink except on Sunday) and about 40 brocante dealers in the square.

Kremlin-Bicetre, Tuesday, Thursday, and Sunday from early morning to about noon on avenue Eugene-Thomas (Porte d'Italie). The market, in a rather grimy working-class neighborhood, is about four blocks more: it is partly in the main boulevard and partly on side streets. Hundreds of vendors mostly sell assorted odds and ends; maybe you'll find something, but it is not as likely as at the markets listed above.

Parking on the street is possible, but you'll probably have to walk several blocks.

Access by Metro to the Porte d'Italie station, then walk south across the boulevard Périphérique.

Porte de Pantin, Marché des Greniers de France, Friday, Saturday, and Sunday mornings (best around 8:30 a. m.). The market has the normal array of bric-a-brac, collectables, and sometimes furniture woven into a fabric of food, clothes, and kitchen gadgets made of plastic, wood, and metal. This is a relatively minor market, and should not be your first choice.

Parking on the street is relatively easy to find compared to most of Paris.

Access by Metro to Porte de Pantin.

Postage Stamp Market, Thursday afternoons and all day Sunday on avenue Gabriel and avenue Marigny, across the street from the Elysées Palace, residence of the President of France.

This is a specialized market strictly devoted to postage stamps. While dozens of dealers and collectors set up tables along the sidewalk and on the gravel and you can find stamps from all over the world, it is unlikely you'll find stamps of great value and rarity.

Street parking in this neighborhood is almost impossible. Public parking is available in the garage on avenue Marigny, just off the Rond-Point des Champs-Elysées.

Access by Metro the Champs-Elysées-Clemenceau station, then walk one block on avenue de Marigny.

## *Paris Auctions*

L'Hôtel Drouot (Hotel Drouot), formally known as the Nouveau Drouot, is France's largest set of auction halls, and is also the center of a several-block area of experts, appraisers, shippers, and dealers. There are several auctions almost every day of the week in several of the the 16 auction halls the Nouveau Drouot.

Many French (and foreign) antique dealers buy their goods here (also less artistic items are sometimes sold here as well, such as appliances, used furniture, even occasionally industrial equipment!). Usually, buyer registration before the sale is required. Payment is required in French francs, either in cash or by check. A buyer's premium is often payable in addition to the sales price.

Many sales are specialized categories: paintings, carpets, furniture, and silver. However, many sales are miscellaneous lots of some furniture, a few paintings, a few glass or crystal items, and other similar collectable or antique items.

Announcements of coming sales are published every Friday in the weekly La Gazette de l'Hôtel Drouot, which is available at the newsstand just inside to the right of the main entrance. Some newsstands in the neighborhood also carry it.

For the schedule of coming sales, you can call a 24-hour recording (in French only) at 47.70.17.17. You can also see a schedule on Teletel (French national computer videotext system) by calling 36.15.91.77 and typing GDROUOT on the keyboard.

Most sales begin at 2 p.m.; inspection of merchandise is usually held the day before from the opening of the doors at 11 a.m. to 5 p.m. (7 p.m. on Thursday), and sometimes also on the day of the sale from 11 a.m. until noon.

In addition to the auctions, many services necessary for the antique trade are found in the building and in neighborhood: shippers, experts and appraisers (some of whom can be of great help when exporting works of art and antiques).

The Hôtel Drouot is located a 9 rue Drouot, Paris 75009, telephone 42.46.17.11. Rue Drouot runs between rue La Fayette and boulevard Montmartre.

Parking is extremely difficult in the vicinity; however, the nearest parking garage (pay) is at the back of the building and entered from rue Chauchat.

The closest Metro stops are Le Peletier, Drouot, and Richelieu.

Crédit Municipal de Paris (municipal pawn shop) holds regular auctions to dispose of pawned and unclaimed items. Quality is variable; you will have to inspect carefully. Sales are organized into categories such as jewelry, books, musical instruments, and "divers"—which means everything else. More sales consist of jewelry (which includes silver, silverware, gold and silver coins, and rings, necklaces, etc.) than anything else. The sales are held at 10:30 a.m. unless otherwise specified in advertising (found in La Gazette de l'Hôtel Drouot and elsewhere), but the days vary. No auctions are held in August. Information can be obtained from the sale site, Crédit Municipal de Paris, 55 rue des Francs- Bourgeouis, 75181 Paris Cedex 04, telephone 42.71.25.43.

Parking in the area is extremely difficult; the nearest parking garages are found near the Beaubourg (Pompidou Center). Enter from the rue de Beaubourg.

The closest Metro stop is Rambuteau, then walk east away from the Pompidou Center for about four blocks.

*Antique Centers*

Le Louvre des Antiquaires (antique dealers' Louvre) is an antique dealers' and antique collectors' dream, though not by any means a flea market. This massive four-story old building was originally opened in 1855 as one of the world's first department stores. After closing as a department store, it reopened with about 250 dealers of some of the most exquisite (and costly) antiques to be found. Not only are the displays wonderful, the setting is classic: a fine skylighted center with silent escalators, polished hardwood floors, soothing music, and clean, free public toilets (south east corner, second floor). Any dealer here should be able to authenticate any item you buy. Even if you can't afford to buy anything, it is a worthwhile browse. The Louvre des Antiquaires open every day except Monday from 11 a.m. to 7 p.m. at 2 place du Palais-Royale, 75001, telephone 42.97.27.00. (Across rue de Rivoli on one side is the Louvre and on the other side across the rue Saint-Honoré is the information office that deal with the exportation of artwork and antiques.)

Parking is almost impossible, though you can on rare occasions find a place to park at the few metered spaces in the square.

Access by Metro is to the Palais Royale station, then walk across the square.

Le Village Suisse (Swiss Village) is another elegant complex of about 150 dealers, on the Left Bank only a short walk from the Eiffel Tower. The shops in this relatively new concrete complex are tiny, but have many exquisite pieces, some of which are of museum quality. Prices here are also quite high and you should be able to obtain certificates of authenticity on almost any purchase made here. This complex is open Thursday through Monday from 11 a.m. to 7 p.m., though because of the layout, you can window-shop on any day of the week. Le Village Suisse has two entrances and two addresses: 78 avenue de Suffren and (around the corner) 54 avenue de la Motte-Picquet.

This is one are of Paris where you may be able to find street parking.

Access by Metro is to la Motte-Picquet or Grenelle stations, then walk one block down the avenue de la Motte-Picquet. Every stand has its own telephone number: there is no central information number.

*Antique Shows*

There are several antique shows in Paris (see also surrounding town listings). The major shows in Paris are listed here.

Biennale Internationale des Antiquaires (International Antique Dealers' Biennale) from the third week of September through the second Sunday of October of even numbered years. It is held at the Grand Palais on the Champs-Elysées at place Clemenceau. This is the largest and most elegant antique show in France. Several hundred antique dealers, mostly French but with a sprinkling of foreign dealers, display all kinds of antiques. Almost all items are of museum quality.

Parking can be difficult. The nearest public parking lot is at the Rond-Point des Champs Elysées, with the entrance on avenue Matignon.

Access by Metro is to the Champs-Elysées Clemenceau station, then walk toward the Seine to find the main entrance. Organized by the French National Antiques dealers association, Syndicat National des Antiquaires, 11 rue Jean-Mermoz, 75008 Paris, telephone 42.25.44.33.

Foire Nationale à la brocante (Please see Chatou).

Foire Internationale à la brocante et de l'antiquité the last week of September and last week of February. It is held at the Parc des Cormailles just outside Paris' city limits in Ivry- sur-Seine. It is one of the largest antiques fairs in France, and coincides with the Chatou fair and the Bienniale in even numbered years. Over 1000 dealers show all kinds of antiques and collectables ranging from glassware and silver plate to furniture. The first two days are reserved for the antiques trade: have a business card or copy of your business license ready. This fair is definitely worth attending.

Access by Metro to the end of the line at the Mairie d'Ivry, then follow the signs and walk downhill to the railway station. Access by RER on Line C to Ivry-sur-Seine (the first station past the city boundary; costs a few francs.) Ample parking is available at the fair site.

Information from Mme. Resse, SODAF, 18 rue Lénine (2 place des Fauconnières), 94200 Ivry-sur-Seine, telephone 46.71.66.14.

## Other Events and Organizers

In addition, about two dozen events are organized by several companies and organizations. Since these markets are subject to change from year to year, contact them when you arrive in France. Generally, they are street fairs, though some are held in various halls and stadiums. These organizations are:

- SADEMA, 17 rue Saint-Paul, 75004 Paris, telephone 48.87.58.48. This company organizes about 15 fairs per year, including the Foire de Brocante de Printemps (Spring Junk Fair) held on avenue Maine around the end of May; Foire de Brocante (Junk Fair) held on Boulevard Blanqui; Brocante de Paris (Paris Junk) at Boulogne-sur-Seine, dates vary; and the Salon d'Antiquites (Antique Salon) at the Eiffel Tower, dates vary.

- O. G. S., 96 rue des Rosiers, 93400 Saint-Ouen, telephone 42.62.44.44. This company organizes two huge junk fairs a year, held in March and in September, the Foire à la Ferraile et aux Jambons.

- Arts-Expo, 10 rue Thenard, 75005 Paris. This company organizes several specialized salons, such as the Paintings and Posters Fair, held in April.

**Pau 64000**

Marché à la brocante (junk market) every Saturday from 7 a.m. to 12 noon and 2 to 6 p.m., and
every Sunday and Monday from 8:30 to noon
at the place de Foirail. This market is in one of
the most lovely of French provincial cities, not
far from the Pyrenees. You'll find items such
as faience from Samadet, items from nearby
Spain, and clay jugs and pots of various types.
Information from the Office de Tourisme, place
Royale, 64000 Pau, telephone 59.27.27.08.


## Perpignan 66000

Marché aux puces (flea market) early Sunday
morning year round at the Parc des Expositions on the avenue de Bompas, the riverbank
street across from the city center. This is probably the largest market on the southern Mediterranean coast, with over 150 regular vendors, but
often the merchandise is disappointing. Look
for forged iron work, domestic clay pottery (especially jugs) bronze statues, and occasionally
faience plates. Information from the Office de
Tourisme, Quai de Lattry- de-Tassigny, 66000
Perpignan, telephone 68.34.29.94.

Salon des Antiquaires du Roussillon (Roussillon antique dealers' salon) in March or April at
the Parc des Expositions (call for exact dates).
This is a smaller and newer fair than many
provincial fairs, mainly featuring local dealers
with a quantities of 19th-century furniture. Organized by the Commisariat Général, 11 rue Allart, 66000 Perpignan, telephone 68.34.73.84.


## Pézenas 34120

Marché aux puces (flea market) every Wednesday morning year round at the place Gambetta. In July and August, the market gets larger
and the antique dealers move to where tourists
can easily find them at the place du Marché-au-
Bled in the town center in front of the church.
This small but ancient town invites antiques to
surface. Wine-related items are common, since
Pézenas is in the largest (if not most famous)

wine-growing areas of France. Information from M. Servieres, Office de Tourisme, place du Marché-au-Bled, 34120 Pézenas, telephone 67.98.11.82.


## Poitiers 86000

Marché aux puces (flea market) every Friday morning (early!) in the place du Marché square around the cathedral. This is the only flea market in the area, and is mixed in with the weekly food and general merchandise market. Specialties you might find include copper basins, and regional ceramics, mostly clay, but including some porcelain. Information from the Office de Tourisme, place Maréchal Leclerc, 86000 Poitiers, telephone 49.01.84.84.

On Pentecost Sunday and the following Monday (five weeks after Easter Sunday, usually in May) and the second week end of December the Foire à la brocante (junk fair) is held at the same location. Information from the tourist office or from the organizer, M. Aldeberg, 15 place Joffre, 86170 Neuville-de- Poitou.

Salon des antiquaires (antique dealers' salon) third weekend of October (including Friday) at the Parc des Expositions, which is about two kilometers east of the city on the autoroute spur, and fronting on rue Salvador Allende. This is a regional fair, with few dealers from outside the region. Information from M. Rullier, 23 rue de l'Ancienne Comedie, 86000 Poitiers.


## Pontoise 95300

Marché à la brocante (junk market) last Sunday of every month (especially in the morning) at place des Maineaux. This market, in the Ile-de-France region, is only 30 kilometers from Paris. Relatively large; you should find collectables and bric-a-brac, but few regional specialties. Information from the Office de Tourisme, 6 place Petit-Martroy, 95300 Pontoise, telephone 30.30.11.91.

Salle des Ventes (public sales hall) auction every Monday and also the last Saturday of every month at 2:30 p.m. The items run to 19th-century furniture and minor paintings, as well as normal glass and porcelain items. Inspection and buyer registration is held the day before and on the morning before the sale. Information from and sales location is Salle des Ventes, 3 bis rue Saint-Martin, 95300 Pontoise, telephone 30.32.01.83.

Salon des antiquaires (antique dealers' salon) in mid-April at the Salle des Fêtes. Since the dates vary, contact the local Office de Tourisme, 6 place Petit-Martroy, 95300 Pontoise, telephone 30.30.11.91, or the organizer, La Crémaillère, 19 rue de Chantilly, 60270 Gouvieux, 44.56.11.60.

## Pont Saint-Esprit 30130

Foire des antiquités et brocante (antique and junk fair) first weekend of July (beginning Friday) at place Saint-Pierre along the Quai de Luynes on the Rhone river in the old town center. Organized by the Comité des Fêtes Antiquités-Brocante, Mairie, 30130 Pont Saint-Esprit, telephone 66.39.90.80 or 66.39.13.25.

Salon des antiquités (antique salon) the four-day weekend around Armistice Day (November 11) at the Salle des Fêtes. This fair's vendors are mostly local and regional dealers with interesting glass, porcelain, but only a small amount of furniture. A small admission fee is charged. Organized by the Comité des Fêtes Antiquités-Brocante, Mairie, 30130 Pont Saint-Esprit, telephone 66.39.90.80 or 66.39.13.25.

## Pornic 44210

Brocante et curiosités (junk and curiosities) the first Sunday of August at the parking lot of the Salle Municipale. This small village near Nantes offers a local sale with some interesting items.

Organized by Mme. Lemercker, Le Porteau, Sainte-Marie-sur-Mer, 44210 Pornic.

## Provins 77160

Marché aux puces (flea market) third Sunday of every month from April to December at the place du Châtel in the partially walled Ville Haute (old upper town). Information from the Office de Tourisme, Tour Cesar, 77160 Provins, telephone 64.00.16.65, or the Comité d'Animation et d'Expansion Artistique, place du Châtel, 77160 Provins.

## Puy

(Please see Le Puy.)

## Reims 51100

Marché aux puces (flea market) first Sunday of the month (except not in August) at the Halles Centrales on the place du Boulingrin, on the north side of the city, only a few hundred meters from the railway station. This market, with about 80 vendors, offers small collectable trinkets. Information from the organizer, Association de Marché aux Puces, Boîte Postale 2118, 51080 Reims Cedex, telephone 26.85.10.71, or 26.87.03.99.

Marché aux puces (flea market) every Saturday and Sunday year round on boulevard Jamin, about 800 meters from the city center on the road to Rethel. This is a food and general merchandise market, whose antique and flea market section is smaller than the once-a-month market. Information from the Office de Tourisme, 3 Boulevard Paix, 51100 Reims, telephone 26.47.04.60.

Salon des antiquaires (antique dealers' salon) at the beginning of October. This is a good regional fair, held at the Foire et Salons de Reims. Organized by La Chambre de Commerce de Reims, Foire et Salons de Reims, 5 rue des Marmouzets, 51100 Reims, telephone 26.40.36.01.

## Rennes 51100

Marché aux puces (flea market) first and third Saturday of the month year round on rue Saint-Georges. The main city of Brittany is a center for furniture restoration and a treasure trove of unrestored furniture, particularly large dark 19th-century pieces such as armoires (which are often more than 8 feet high).

Salon des antiquaires (antique dealers' salon) last weekend of September. This is a regional show, but since the location is subject to change, contact the organizers: Prom'art, 9 rue Offenbach, 35100 Rennes, telephone 99.50.74.19.

## Rochelle

(Please see La Rochelle.)

## Romans-sur-Isère 26100

Marché à la brocante (junk market) first Saturday of the month at the market hall along the Isère River on Quai Chopin. This market is part of the regular food and general merchandise market. Information from the Office de Tourisme, place J.-Nadi, 26100 Romans-sur-Isère, telephone 75.02.28.72.

## Roubaix 59100

(Please also see Lille 59000.)

Marché aux puces (flea market) every Sunday from 9 a.m. to noon at the parking garage at 30 rue des Fabricants. This market, in grimy brick factory town almost on the Belgian border, has about 50 sellers (more when it rains, because the market is indoors) and is worth visiting after the larger Marché de Wazemmes in nearby Lille. Similar items are sold. Information from the Office de Tourisme, Mairie (City Hall), 59100 Roubaix, telephone 20.79.70.02.

**Rouen 76000**

The capital city of the opulent province of Normandy, Rouen is rich in antiques and collectables as well as old half-timbered houses and an ancient astronomical clock. It is a region still rich in many types of antiques, though sellers usually know the value of what they sell.

Marché aux puces (flea market) every Saturday and Sunday (early!) at the Clos Saint-Marc, near the church of Saint-Maclou in the city center. This is the largest market in the area with about 100 vendors. You're likely to find various bibelots and collectables. This is part of the largest public market (some of which is indoors) in Rouen. Information from the Office de Tourisme, 25 place Cathédrale, 76000 Rouen, telephone 35.71.41.77.

Marché aux puces (flea market) first Wednesday of every month on rue Eau-de-Robec, near the church of Saint- Ouen, slightly east of the city's central rue de la République. This monthly market attracts many browsers as well as vendors, more in sunny weather than rain. Usual collectables and antiques abound, but watch for reproductions, especially pottery. Information from the Office de Tourisme, 25 place Cathédrale, 76000 Rouen, telephone 35.71.41.77.

Marché aux puces (flea market) every Wednesday at place des Emmures. This is part of a regular food and general merchandise market and is less interesting than the other regular markets because there are fewer antiques. Information from the Office de Tourisme, 25 place Cathédrale, 76000 Rouen, telephone 35.71.41.77.

Foire à la Ferraille (junk iron fair), the fourth Sunday and Monday of June on the rue de Robec and most of the Saint-Maclou district. This fair, which offers far more than junk iron, is the one of the largest flea markets in France. Hundreds of vendors offer both used and old goods and new items as well. Information is available from the organizer, Mme. T. Cleon, 164 rue Eau-de-Robec, 76000 Rouen, telephone 35.88.63.16.

Salon des antiquaires (antique dealers' salon) at the end of April and beginning of May (dates shift slightly from year to year) from 2 to 10 p.m., except 10 a.m. to 10 p.m. on weekends and May Day (May 1, a national holiday). It takes place at the Halle aux Toilles. Some 100 dealers, mainly from the region, offer much of the best of fruitwood furniture, glass, crystal, faience, pottery, and silver. Prices match the relatively high quality. Information from the organizer, Mme. Popelin, 20 rue Saint-Romain, 76000 Rouen, telephone 35.71.35.06.

Salon national des antiquaires (national antique dealers' salon) from the second to the third week of October at the Parc des Expositions. This is one of the major antique shows in France, with a regional emphasis. Some Parisian dealers also exhibit and buy at this fair. Prices are high but only true antiques (mostly of high quality) are sold. Information from the Groupe des Salons Sélectionées d'Antiquaires, Boulevard de Champagne, Boîte Postale 108, 21003 Dijon Cedex, telephone 80.71.44.34, or the local organizer, M. Asseline, COMET, Boîte Postale 1080, 76016 Rouen Cedex, telephone 35.66.52.52.

## Royan 17200

Marché aux puces (flea market) every Sunday of July and August. This summer market is put together for the tourists flocking to this summer seaside resort. Information from the Office de Tourisme, Palais des Congrès (near the yacht harbor) 17200 Royan, telephone 46.38.65.11.

Marché de la brocante (junk market) every Wednesday and Saturday morning of July and

August at La Tache Vert. This summer
market, like the Sunday flea market, is put on
for the pleasure of the thousands of tourists. Information from the Office de Tourisme, Palais
des Congrès (near the yacht harbor) 17200
Royan, telephone 46.38.65.11.

## Royat  63130

(Please see Clermont-Ferrand.)

## Sables d'Olonne 85100

(Please see Les Sables d'Olonne.)

## Saint-Brieuc 22000

Salle des Ventes (public auction hall) auction
every Tuesday at 2 p.m. Registration Saturday,
Monday, and just before the sale begins. This
auction is one of the better places to buy old
Breton furniture, old books, and nautical
items. Catalogues are sometimes available
several weeks before the most important sales.
Information from the Salle des Ventes 16 rue
Vicairie,        22000        Saint-Brieuc,        telephone
96.33.15.91.

Foire à la brocante et aux antiquités (antique
and junk fair) first weekend of December (including Friday) at the Parc de Brézillet. This is a
regional fair, where you may find Breton antiques. Information from the Foire des Côtes
d'Armor, Boîte Postale 236, Parc de Brézillet,
22004 Saint-Brieuc Cedex.

## Saint-Ètienne 42000

Marché aux puces (flea market) every Sunday
morning year round (starts early) on boulevard
Jules-Janin, near the railway viaduct, Gare Carnot, and the Parc des Expositions on the north
side of the city. This is the largest flea market in
this part of central France; you're likely to find

faience and domestic pottery, open copper basins and especially iron cauldrons, andirons, and fireplace pokers. Information from the Office de Tourisme, 12 rue Gérentet, 42000 Saint-Ètienne, telephone 77.25.12.14 (closed Sunday and Monday).

Marché à la brocante (junk market) second Saturday of every month year round on the "Plate-forme" level of the parking garage on the rue des Ursulines in the city center. Similar items can be found at the Sunday market, but here it isn't mixed in with food and new items. Organized by the Association Promotion Brocante, 3 place Grenette, 42000 Saint- Ètienne, telephone 77.32.66.46.

Salon en Forez des antiquaires et brocanteurs (Forez antique and junk dealers' salon) for 10 days at the beginning of November at the Palais des Expositions on boulevard Jules-Janin. During the rest of the year, many of these dealers have permanent galleries, at which information can be obtained. Contact M. Verney, Groupement d'Intérêt Economique Antiquaires de Forez, rue de la Richelandière, 42100 Saint-Ètienne, telephone 77.32.65.49.

### Saint-Fons 69190

Marché aux puces (flea market) every Sunday morning year round beginning about an hour past dawn on boulevard Sampaix. The market here, part of a general food and miscellaneous merchandise market, is refreshing after nearby Lyons' monstrous and crowded markets. The selection is much smaller—don't plan to find lots of antiques here.

### Saint-Georges-les-Baillargeaux 86130

Marché à la brocante (junk market) first Saturday of every month at place de l'Eglise. This small town in west central France offers about two dozen vendors of odds and ends, including old copper and iron pots, wood and iron farm implements, and sometimes traditional pottery.

## Saint-Germain-en-Laye 78100

Salle des Ventes (public sales hall) auction every Wednesday at 10 a.m. and 2 p.m. and every Sunday at 2 p.m. This Parisian suburb has a fine selection at close to Parisian prices. Expect high finish and elegance rather than rustic country items. Information and sale site is Salle des Ventes, 9 rue des Arcades, 78100 Saint-Germain-en-Laye, telephone 39.73.95.64.

Salon des antiquaires (antique dealers' salon) the end of April to beginning of May (changes yearly) at the Manège Royal. This relatively small show is close to Paris; selection and prices are also similar. Information from Expotrolles-Margeridon, 171 rue du Faubourg Saint-Antoine, 75011 Paris.

## Saint-Girons 09200

Foire aux antiquités et à la brocante (antique and junk dealers' fair) second week of August in the town center. This is the major annual event of the region. Information from Foire aux Antiquités, Boîte Postale 30, 09200 Saint-Girons, telephone 61.66.04.00.

## Saint-Tropez 83990

Marché aux puces (flea market) every Tuesday and Saturday morning about 8 a.m. on the place des Lices in this elegant resort village. The antiques and junk are mixed in with the vegetables and souvenirs; because of the large extent of the tourist trade, don't expect to make great finds at this market. Information from Mme. Yalaine Hery, Syndicat d'Initiative de Bormes, rue Jean Ricard, 83230 Bormes-les-Mimosas, telephone 94.71.15.17.

Salon des antiquaires (antique dealers' salon) last Thursday of August to the second Sunday in

September at the place des Lices. More than 100 dealers offer antiques and genuine items only. This is a good show, where you can find Provençal furniture and minor paintings, glassware, and occasional wood carvings. The first day (Thursday) is reserved for dealers only: have a business card and maybe a copy of a business license ready. For information, contact the M. Julien, Office Culturel et d'Animation de Saint-Tropez, Mairie, 83990 Saint-Tropez, telephone 94.97.00.13.


## Saint-Vit 25410

Marché à la brocante (junk market) second Sunday of each month from March through October from 8 a.m. to 1 p.m. This is a relatively small, country-style market in rustic surroundings in the town center.


## Samatan 32130

Salon des antiquaires (antique dealers' salon) fourth weekend and following Monday of August at place de la Mairie in the village center. This is a major regional fair. (Dealers' day is on Friday—bring some business cards or copy of your business license and you're in.) Organized by the Association des Commerçants et Artisans de Samaton, Axe Toulouse-Lombez, place de la Mairie, 32130 Samatan, telephone 62.62.31.58.


## Samoise-sur-Seine 77920

Marché de brocante (junk market) last Sunday of every month except December. This is a relatively small market in the distant outskirts of Paris near Fontainebleau. The market is much smaller the last weekend of June. Information from ABSEM, 100 rue Général de Gaulle, 77780 Bourron-Marlotte.

## Savigny-sur-Orge 91600

Marché aux puces (flea market) first Saturday of the month year round at place Davault and second Saturday of the month as part of the market at the adjoining Marché au Plateau.

## Seine-Port 77113

Petit marché aux puces (little flea market) first Sunday of every month except January and September at the place des Tilleuls. This market is close enough to Paris to be influenced by Parisian styles and also prices. Fewer than 50 vendors offer all kinds of odds and ends.

## Semur-en-Auxois 21140

Salle des Ventes (public auction house) auction every Sunday at 2 p.m. Inspection and buyer registration take place before the sale begins. Information and sale at the Salle des Ventes, 18 rue du Rempart, 21140 Semur-en-Auxois, telephone 80.97.20.90.

## Seyne 83500

(Please see La Seyne 83500.)

## Soisy-sous-Montmorency 95230

Marché aux puces (flea market) Wednesday, Saturday, and Sunday year round on avenue de la Division Leclerc. This market, far enough out from Paris to be away from its direct influence, is part antiques and used goods, but even more a food and new merchandise market.

## Soumolou 64420

Marché aux puces (flea market) first Sunday of the month year round in the town center. This is one of the small regional markets along the Pyrenees in southern France.


## Strasbourg 67000

Marché aux puces (flea market) Wednesday and Saturday year round from about 7:30 a.m. at the place de l'Viel Hôpital. This picturesque district in one of France's most graceful cities provides a wonderful setting to find old stoneware crocks and butter churns, but only a small amount of solid silver, glasses and wine carafes, and porcelains. Because Strasbourg was part of Germany from 1871 to 1918, be familiar with German hallmarks and expect to see some German porcelains. While the general price level is higher than in much of France, it is lower than nearby Germany for pieces of equivalent quality. Information from the Service Municipal de Droits de place, Hôtel de Ville, 67000 Strasbourg, telephone 88.84.90.90.

Marché aux puces (flea market) every Saturday and Sunday in the place du Château just south of the cathedral in the old city center. Parking is impossible in this neighborhood; you'll have to park across the river or the underground parking lot at place Gutenberg. This market is much more designed for tourists than the other market. Information from the Service Municipal de Droits de place, Hôtel de Ville, 67000 Strasbourg, telephone 88.84.90.90.

Carrefour européen de l'antiquité (European antiques crossroads) show in mid January at the Parc des Expositions du Wacken. This is a major regional antique show and sale, though there are foreign exhibitors and buyers, particularly from nearby Germany. Organized by Prom'Art, 4 rue Offenbach, 35100 Rennes, telephone 99. 50.74.19, or the local representative, M. Chenkier, telephone 88.32.82.76.

Exposition d'antiquités (antiques show) the end of April and beginning of May at the Parc des Expositions du Wacken. This is a solely regional show. Information from SOFEX, Parc des Expositions du Wacken, 67000 Strasbourg.

## Tarbes 65000

Marché à la brocante (junk market) first Saturday of every month year round beginning about 8:30 a.m. to late afternoon at the Halle Marcadieu at place Marcadieu in the center of town. This is a large regional market; local specialties sometimes found include wood carvings, old jewelry and clocks, milk jugs, boxes, and spoons. Information from the Syndicat d'Initiative, place Verdun, 65000 Tarbes, telephone 62.93.36.62.

Marché aux puces (flea market) every Thursday from early morning to noon at place Marcadieu as part of the food and general merchandise market. Information from the Syndicat d'Initiative, place Verdun, 65000 Tarbes, telephone 62.93.36.62.

## Teich 33470

Salon des antiquaires du bassin d'Arcachon (Archachon basin antique dealers' salon) the week of Bastille Day (July 14) throughout this suburb's center in the vicinity of Bordeaux. About 50 exhibitors show regional antiques. Information from the Mairie du Teich, 33470 Teich, telephone 56.22.88.09.

## Thionville 57100

Marché aux puces (flea market) second Saturday of every month year round (beginning just after dawn) on rue de Manège Prolongée and adjoining place de la Liberté, in the center of town. This relatively large market is one of the older ones. You may occasionally find interesting glass, faience, and occasionally small silver and silver plate items. Information from the Office de Tourisme, 16 rue Vieux Collège, 57100 Thionville, telephone 82.53.33.18.

## Thiviers 24800

Marché aux puces (flea market) the weekend
closest to Bastille Day (July 14) and also the
second weekend of August in the Parc Municipal
of this small town in Perigord. These are fine,
rural markets, with a predominance of folk art.
Though few American or Canadian tourists frequent this part of France, this is prime tourist
country for the French and other Europeans. Information from the Syndicat d'Initiative, place
Maréchal Foch, 24800 Thiviers, telephone
53.55.12.50.

## Thouars 79100

Foire des antiquités et de la brocante (antique
and junk fair) second Friday through following
Monday of April at Square Franklin Roosevelt.
This regional country fair in a quiet country
town is enjoyable; exhibitors bring regional
items such as glass, wood carvings, faience,
and clocks. Organized by the Comité de la
Foire du 15 avril, Mairie du Thouars, 79100
Thouars, telephone 49.68.11.11.

## Tonnerre 89700

Salon des antiquaires et brocanteurs (antique
and junk dealers' salon) first Friday to following Sunday at the Viel' Hôpital. This major
regional show offers wine trade items and
dark, massive provincial furniture. Information
from the Office de Tourisme, place Marguerite
de Bourgogne, 89700 Tonnerre, telephone
86.55.14.48, or from the organizer, M. Dubois,
5 avenue de Genève, 74160 Saint-Julien-en-
Genevois, telephone 50.49.27.40.

## Toulon 83100

Marché aux puces (flea market) every Sunday
morning in the Quartier Sainte-Musse at the

Parking Dutasta. This market is on the eastern side of the city, in the area of the sports arena and not far from the Gare Maritime. This market attracts lots of Arabs. You may find some items of Algerian origin, as well as quantities of maritime and fishing gear. Finds can be made at this market, in part because the region is economically depressed and is far off the usual tourist paths. Organized by the Mairie de Toulon, Hôtel de Ville, 83100 Toulon, telephone 94.46.90.46.

Salon International Indépendant de l'Antiquité (International Independent Antique Salon) at the Parc des Expositions in July, centered on Bastille Day (July 14). This is a relatively small regional fair. Information from Var Expansion, Parc des Expositions de Sainte-Musse, 83058 Toulon.

## Toulouse 31000

Marché aux puces (flea market) Saturday and Monday from 8 a.m. to 6 p.m. and Sunday from 8 a.m. to noon, in place Saint-Sernin, facing Basilique Saint-Sernin. This is a large market in a lively city; specialties you may find here include turn-of-the century art work of all types, including bronze statues, paintings, and sculpture; brass door knobs, door knockers, and hinges; and late 19th-century glassware. Organized by the Ville de Toulouse, Mairie, Direction des Droits de Stationnement, 30148 Toulouse Cedex, telephone 61.22.23.72.

Brocante de Printemps (spring junk fair) from the first Wednesday through the following Sunday of March at the Parc des Expositions, in the park on the island in the middle of the Garonne river. This is a major market, with about 150 vendors, who are mostly full-time dealers. Organized by Sforman S. A., 31 rue du Rempart-Matabieu, 31000 Toulouse, telephone 61.21.93.25 or 61.21.81.26.

Salon des antiquaires de Languedoc-Midi-Pyrénées (Languedoc-Midi-and Pyrenees antique dealers' salon) first Thursday through second Sunday of November at the Parc des Expositions, on the island in the Garonne river. This is one of the major antique fairs of France: over 500 dealers from many areas of France sell their wares. Experts and appraisers are available. An admission charge is collected from visitors. Organized by Sforman S. A., 31 rue du Rempart-Matabieu, 31000 Toulouse, telephone 61.21.93.25 or 61.21.81.26.

## Tournus 71700

Salon des antiquaires (antique dealers' salon) fourth Sunday of May until the first Sunday of June in the beautiful, historic and well-preserved district around the Romanesque Abbey of Saint-Philibert. This is a good sized regional sale, where you may find old baskets, wickerwork, vineyard and wine trade items, and occasional pieces of Burgundian walnut furniture. Information from the Office de Tourisme, place Carnot, 71700 Tournus, telephone 85.51.13.10, or the organizer, M. Schenck, 23 rue du Centre, 71700 Tournus.

## Tours 37000

Marché aux puces (flea market) Wednesday and Saturday mornings year round at place de la Victoire, near the food market on the western side of the old city center. The market has depth, but there are few local specialty items aside from faience. This area is full of junk shops with broken-down furniture and gold 19th-century items. Information from the Office de Tourisme, place Maréchal Leclerc, 37000 Tours, telephone 47.05.58.08.

Salon des antiquaires (antique dealers' salon) in mid-March. This regional show moves from place to place: contact the organizers for details. Information from Prom'Art, 4 rue Offenbach, 35100 Rennes, telephone 99.50.74.19.

## Trouville-sur-Mer 14360

Salons des antiquaires (antique dealers' salons) twice a year for 10 days, beginning May 1 and November 1 at the casino. This is an elegant small show at a classic summer resort along the Atlantic shore. Information from the organizers at the Casino de Trouville, place du Maréchal Foch, 14360 Trouville- sur-Mer, telephone 31.88.76.09.

## Troyes 10000

Marché aux puces (flea market) Saturday morning at place Saint Rémy, and adjoining rue Passerat. This vibrant market in an untouristed but picturesque city is interesting. There are finds to be made, especially in heavy provincial furniture, wood and stone carvings, and rustic pictures. This market is part of the regular Saturday food and general market. Information from the Office de Tourisme, 16 boulevard Carnot, 10000 Troyes, telephone 25.73.00.36.

Marché de la brocante (junk market) second Sunday of every month year round at the place de la Cathédrale in the city center. This market is strictly for antiques and junk but no new items or food. Information from the Office de Tourisme, 16 boulevard Carnot, 10000 Troyes, telephone 25.73.00.36.

Salon des antiquaires (antique dealers' salon) the first weekend of May (starting on Friday) every year at the Parc des Expositions on the boulevard de Belgique. This is the major antiques event of the region, with dozens of dealers and some on- site expert appraisers. Free parking is available in a large lot across the street. Information is available from M. Robert Richard, Route Sens-Troyes, Le Mineroy, 10160 Aix-en-Outhe, telephone 25.40.72.69.

## Tulle 19000

Salon des antiquités et de la brocante (antique and junk salon) Easter Sunday and the following Monday at the Centre Culturel et Sportif, near the railway station. This minor regional fair in a poor region of France is interesting for the ambiance, and you may find occasional pieces of folk art. Information from the Office de Tourisme, Quai Baluze, 19000 Tulle, telephone 55.26.59.61.

## Ury  77116

Marché d'antiquités et brocante le Cheval Blanc (White Horse antique and junk market) every Saturday and Sunday from 10 a.m. to 8 p.m. about 10 kilometers south of Fontainebleau (take Autoroute A6, exit at Route Nationale 152, and follow RN 152 to the intersection of D63). Parking is available, but this market cannot be reached on public transit. Organized by M. Robert Paillard, 77116 Ury, telephone 64.24.44.47.

## Valence 26000

Marché aux puces (flea market) first Sunday morning of every month at place Saint-Jean, in and around the market hall. Information from the Mairie de Valence, avenue Félix Faure, 26000 Valence, telephone 75.43.93.00.

Salon des antiquaires et brocanteurs (antique and junk dealers' salon) second weekend of November at the Palais de la Foire. This fair is especially strong in antique cars and old automotive items. Information from the Office de Tourisme, avenue Félix Faure, 26000 Valence, telephone 75.43.04.88, or from the organizer, M. Dubois, 5 avenue de Genève, 74160 Saint-Julien-en- Genevois, telephone 50.49.27.40.

**Vannes 56000**

Marché aux puces (flea market) first Saturday of
the month year round from 8 a.m. to 4 p.m.
around and in front of the church of Saint-
Patern about 100 meters outside the city gate.
Information from the Office de Tourisme, 29 rue
Thiers, 56000 Vannes, telephone 97.47.24.34.

Hôtel des Ventes (public sales hall) auction every
Saturday year round at 2 p.m.   This auction
often has old Breton furniture, and religious
jewelry and wood carvings. Information and
buyer registration is held Friday from 9 a.m. to
noon, and from 2 to 6:30 p.m., and Saturday
morning. Information and sale location is Hôtel
des Ventes de Vannes, 9 rue Saint- Gruenhael
(in the town center), 56000 Vannes, telephone
97.47.26.32.


**Vatan 36150**

Foire à la brocante (junk fair) fourth Sunday of
September (starts early!) on the rue des Récol-
lets. This minor market in a small village in
the center of France is small, but may be
worthwhile if you're already in the area. Organized by M. Pourchasse, 24 rue F. Charbon-
nier, 36150 Vatan.


**Vendôme 41100**

Petit marché aux puces (small flea market)
Thursday morning as part of the general
market. Only about half a dozen vendors offer
a miscellany of junk and second-hand items;
the rest of the market is given over to food,
clothes, tools, etc. The first weekend of September, there are about 40 dealers offering junk and
other odds and ends. Information from the Office
de Tourisme, rue Poterie, 41100 Vendôme,
telephone 54.77.05.07.

## Verdun 55100

Salle des Ventes (public sales hall) auction every
Saturday at 2 p.m. Sometimes beautiful woodwork articles and furniture appear on the auction block. Inspection and buyer registration
takes place before the sale. Information and
sales at the Salle des Ventes, 1 place de la Gare,
55100 Verdun, telephone 29.86.24.67.

Foire aux antiquités (antique fair) in mid-
February in the Zone Industrielle on the Route
d'Etain. This small regional fair isn't worth a
special trip: you're likely to find typical Lorraine
items, and occasional souvenirs of the World
War I battle fought on the ridge just east of
town. Information from M. Baugnon, Mairie,
place Belle-Vierge, 55100 Verdun.

## Versailles 78000

Petit marché aux puces (little flea market) every
Saturday and Sunday from 9:30 a.m. until 7 p.m.
on Passage de la Geôle, behind the Eglise Notre-
Dame in the angle of boulevard de la Reine
and rue Rameau. This passage has outdoor ven-
dors as well as regular merchants indoors. You'll
find minor jewelry, arms, books, and occasional
Oriental pieces. Information from Passage et
Cour des Antiquaires, 10 rue Rameau, 78000
Versailles, telephone 39.53.84.96.

Salon des antiquaires (antique dealers' salon)
at beginning of June, at the Orangerie of the
Chateau. This salon attempts to recreate the
great century of Versailles: rather nice pieces are
shown here (at rather high prices). Organized by
S. O. P. A., 14 Route de Nantes, 44650 Legé.

## Vervins 02140

Salle des Ventes (public sales hall) auction Wednesday and Fridays from 2:30 p.m. to 7 p.m. and
Saturday from 10 a.m. to noon. Inspection of
items to be sold and buyer registration is held
before the sale begins. Information and sales at

the Salle des Ventes, 8 rue de la Republique, 02140 Vervins.

## Villefranche-du-Périgord 24550

Foire à la brocante (junk fair) last weekend of August throughout this small, picturesque town. It is to some degree a tourist attraction, but the fair has some rustic furniture and farm items from about 60 vendors, mostly dealers. An authorized expert is on the fair site, who will assess antiques and informally appraise items for no charge. Information from the M. Issard, Syndicat d'Initiative, Mairie, 24550 Villefranche-du-Périgord, telephone 53.29.91.44.

## Villeneuve-les-Avignon 30400

(Please also see Avignon.)

Salon des antiquaires (antique dealers' salon) first Friday through second Sunday of September at the Chartreuse de Val de Bénédiction. This major regional elegant show is juried: only dealers may exhibit and only antiques may be sold. No reproductions are permitted. Information from M. Michel Joubert, Mairie de Villeneuve-les-Avignon, 30400 Villeneuve-les- Avignon, telephone 90.25.42.03.

## Vire 14500

Hôtel des Ventes (public sales hall) every Saturday at 2:30 p.m. and occasionally on Sundays as well. Inspection and buyer registration is before the sale begins. Information from the Hôtel des Ventes, 4 rue du Cotin, 14500 Vire, telephone 31.68.17.19.

## Vitry-le-François 51300

Salle des Ventes (public sales hall) auction the first and third Monday of every month at 2 p.m. Inspection of merchandise and buyer registration is held before the sale begins. Information from the Salle des Ventes, 9 Faubourg Léon-Bourgeois, 51300 Vitry-le-François, telephone 26.74.75.02.

## Vittel 88800

Salon vosgien des antiquaires (Vosges region antique dealers' salon) Friday through Monday at Pentecost (the fifth Sunday after Easter—often in May) at the Palais de Congrès. This is one of the largest regional fairs in Lorraine; dealers show only original items such as furniture, glassware, crystal, and copper. Reproductions are strictly forbidden. Appraisers are on duty.

This turn-of-the-century thermal resort has clearly seen better days, but to visit Vittel is to see engaging an snapshot of earlier times. Information from Mme. Jackie Français, 180 rue Division Leclerc, 88800 Vittel, telephone 29.08.47.91.

## Xaronval (Charmes) 88130

Foire vosgienne de brocante à Xaronval (Vosges junk fair at Xaronval) the last weekend of September, near the village of Charmes. This is a regional fair with perhaps 50 dealers trying to sell their items. Information from M. Lacourt, Xaronval, 88130 Charmes, telephone 29.66.12.41.

# Major Annual and Biannual Markets, Shows, and Antiques Events

Many major antiques trade events take place once or twice a year, some once every two years. Additional details for each event below are found in the alphabetical listings in the book; you may wish to plan your journey to coincide with these major fairs and shows. Not every show is listed.

This brief calendar listing is divided by month with cities alphabetically listed within each month.

## January

Bordeaux: Salon des antiquaires de Bordeaux-Lainè, mid-January.

Enghien-les-Bains: Foire d'antiquités et brocante, mid-January.

Grenoble: Salon Européen des antiquaires, end of January and beginning of February.

Strasbourg: Carrefour eurepéen de l'antiquité, mid-January.

## February

Avignon: Salon des antiquaires, second week of February.

Béziers: Salon des antiquaires, first weekend of February.

Bordeaux: Salon des antiquaires Bordeaux-Lac, second week of February.

Bourges: Journèes de l'Antiquité, second weekend of February.

Verdun: Foire aux antiquités, mid February.

## March

Beaune: Salon des antiquaires et brocanteurs, last weekend of March or first weekend of April.

Chatou (near Paris): Foire nationale à la brocante, beginning of March.

Nîmes: Journées Nationales de la Brocante, beginning of March.

Orleans: Foire aux antiquités et à la paperasse, second week of March.

Toulouse: Brocante de Printemps, first Wednesday through following Sunday of March.

Tours: Salon des antiquaires, mid March.

## April

Barjac: Foire de Barjac, Easter Sunday and following Monday.

Chalons-sur-Marne: Salon des antiquaires, first weekend of April.

Crozon: Foire à la brocante, first week of April.

Le Mans: 24 heures de la brocante, second weekend of April.

L'Isle-sur-Sorgue: Foire à brocante, Easter week and the Monday after Easter.

Montpellier: Salon des antiquaires et de la brocante, 25th of April through second Sunday of May.

Nancy: Salon des Antiquités, mid April.

Nevers: Foire à la brocante, second half of April.

Perpignan: Salon des antiquaires du Roussillon, third week of April (1987), some other years last week of March.

Pontoise: Salon des antiquaires, mid April.

Rouen: Salon des antiquaires, end of April and beginning of May.

Strasbourg: Exposition d'Antiquités, end of April and beginning of May.

Thouars: Foire des antiquités et de la brocante, second Friday through following Monday of April.

Tulle: Salon des antiquités, Easter Sunday and following Monday.

## May

Chalons-sur-Marne: Salon des antiquaires et brocanteurs, third week of May.

Colmar: Salon des antiquaires, first weekend of May.

Dijon: Salon des antiquaires et de la brocante, two weeks in May.

Eauze: Salon des antiquaires, first half of May.

Meyrargues: Foire des brocanteurs, end of May or beginning of June.

Obernai: Foire à la brocante, second week of May.

Orange: Salon des antiquaires, last Friday of May through second Sunday following.

Poitiers: Foire à la brocante, Pentecost Sunday and the following Monday.

Saint-Germain-en-Laye: Salon des antiquaires, end of April to beginning of May.

Tournus: Salon des antiquaires, fourth Sunday of May through first Sunday of June.

Trouville-sur-Mer: Salon des antiquaires, May 1 through May 10.

Troyes: Salon des antiquaires, first weekend of May.

Vittel: Salon Vosgien des antiquaires, Friday through Sunday at Pentecost (usually in May).

## June

Aigues-Mortes 30220: Foire à la brocante, third weekend of June.

Caen: Salon des antiquaires, second weekend to third weekend of June.

Magny-en-Vexin:    Salon    d'antiquités    et brocante, mid-June.

Mantes-la-Jolie: Foire de brocante, last weekend of June.

Orange: (Please see May)

Rouen: Foire à la Ferraille, fourth Sunday and Monday of June.

Versailles: Salon des antiquaires, beginning of June.

## July

Apt: Foire à la brocante, last weekend in July through following Tuesday.

Cusset: Salon des antiquaires et de la brocante, second week of July.

Guerande: Salon des antiquaires, third week of July.

Mirande: Salon des antiquaires, week of Bastille Day (July 14).

Mouans-Sartoux: Foire à la brocante, third weekend of July.

Pont Saint-Esprit: Foire des Antiquités et brocante, first weekend of July.

Teich: Salon des antiquaires du bassin d'Arcachon, week of Bastille Day (July 14).

Thiviers: Marché aux puces, weekend closest to Bastille Day (July 14).

Toulon: Salon International Indépendant de l'Antiquité, week of Bastille Day (July 14).

**August**

Annecy: Salon d'antiquités de la rentrée, end of August.

Barjac: Foire de Barjac, Assumption Day holiday (August 15 and adjoining days).

Corbielle-Essones (near Paris): Foire à la brocante, August 15 (Assumption Day).

Divonne-les-Bains: Grande foire aux antiquaires et brocanteurs, third weekend of August.

Fayence: Foire de la brocante, first weekend of August.

Gerardmer: Salon des antiquaires et brocanteurs, first weekend of August.

Gien: Foire des antiquités et brocante, fourth weekend of August.

Guerande: Salon des antiquaires, Assumption Day (August 15) week.

L'Isle-sur-Sorgue: Foire à la brocante, Assumption Day (August 15) weekend.

Luxieul-les-Bains: Grande foire aux antiquaires et brocanteurs, last weekend of August.

Pornic: Brocante et curiosités, first Sunday of August.

Saint-Girons: Foire aux antiquités et à la brocante, second week of August.

Saint-Tropez: Salon des antiquaires, last Thursday of August to second Sunday in September.

Samatan: Salon des antiquaires, fourth weekend of August and the following Monday.

Thiviers: Marché aux puces, second weekend of August.

Villefranche-du-Périgord: Foire à la brocante, last weekend of August.


## September

Arles: Salon des antiquaires et de la brocante, last week of September.

Auch: Salon des antiquaires, first 15 days of September.

Bar-le-Duc: Salon des antiquaires, second week of September.

Bourg-en-Bresse: Salon des antiquaires, second and third week of September.

Charmes: La Foire Vosgienne des brocanteurs, last weekend of September.

Chatou (near Paris): Foire nationale à la brocante, end of September.

Compiègne: Salon des antiquaires, second Thursday through following Sunday of September.

Contrexèville: Salon des antiquaires et brocanteurs, first weekend of September.

Dijon: Foire à la brocante, mid-September.

Durtal: Grande rendez-vous de la brocante, last Sunday in September.

Etampes: Salon des antiquaires, mid-September.

Haguenau: Salon des antiquaires et brocanteurs, second weekend of September.

Orléans: Salon d'Automne des antiquaires, end of September and beginning of October.

Paris: Biennale Internationale des antiquaires, third week of September through second Sunday of October.

Paris—Ivry-sur-Seine: Internationale de l'antiquité et à la brocante, last week of September.

Rennes: Salon des antiquaires, last weekend of September.

Vatan: Foire à la brocante, fourth Sunday of September.

Villeneuve-des-Avignon: Salon des antiquaires, first Friday through second September of September.

## October

Aix-en-Provence: Salon des antiquaires, first two weeks of the month.

Albi: Foire à la brocante et aux antiquaires, first weekend in September.

Besançon: Salon Comptoise des antiquaires, first week of October.

Guingamp: Foire à la brocante, fourth weekend of October.

Lamorlaye: Exposition d'antiquaires, during October.

Lille: Bienniale de l'antiquité: second weekend of October in odd numbered years.

Marseille: Salon des antiquaires, third week of October.

Obernai: Foire à la brocante, October 32 through November 2.

Poitiers: Salon des antiquaires, third weekend of October.

Reims: Salon des antiquaires, beginning of October.

Rouen: Salon national des antiquaires, second to third week of October.

Tonnerre: Salon des antiquaires et brocanteurs, first weekend of October.

## November

Metz: Salon des antiquaires, fourth week of November.

Pont Saint-Esprit: Salon des antiquités, four-day weekend around Armistice Day (November 11).

Saint-Étienne: Salon en Forez des antiquaires et brocanteurs, beginning of November.

Toulouse: Salon des antiquaires de Languedoc-Midi- Pyrénées, first Thursday through following Sunday of November.

Trouville-sur-Mer: Salon des antiquaires, November 1 through 10.

Valence: Salon des antiquaires et brocanteurs, second weekend of November.


## December

Angoulême: Salon des antiquaires, first weekend of December.

Béziers: Salon des antiquaires, first weekend of December.

Mâcon: Foire à la brocante, first weekend of December.

Montauban: Salon des antiquaires et brocanteurs de Quercy, first Thursday through following Sunday of December.

Nîmes: Salon des antiquaires et brocanteurs, second week of December.

Poitiers: Foire à la brocante, second weekend of December.

Saint-Brieuc: Foire à la brocante et aux antiquités, first weekend of December.

# Auctions City by City

Many cities and towns in France have regularly scheduled auctions. Most take place in public sales halls ("Salle des Ventes"). Here is a list of towns with days and hours of sales. Viewing is held before the sales begin.

Angers, Tuesday, 2 p.m.
Auxerre, Friday, 2 p.m.
Avignon, Thursday, 9 a.m.

Bayeux, every Saturday (occasionally Sunday), 2:30 p.m.
Bolbec, two Saturdays per month, 2 p.m.
Bordeaux (Hôtel des Ventes), Thursday, 2:30 p.m.
Brive-la-Gaillarde, Saturday, 2 p.m.

Calais, Friday and Sunday, 2:30 p.m.
Chalon-sur-Saône, Thursday and Saturday, 2 p.m.
Chartres (Hôtel des Ventes), Tuesday and Saturday, 2 p.m.
Chinon, Monday, 2 p.m.

Deauville, Saturday, 10 a.m. and 2 p.m.
Dieppe, Saturday, 12:30 p.m.
Dijon, Wednesday and Sunday, 2 p.m.

Enghien-les-Baines, twice a month (call for dates and times).
Etampes, Sunday, 2 p.m.

Fontainebleau, Wednesday morning, Saturday and Sunday afternoon.

Granville, Saturday and Sunday, 2:30 p.m.

Joigny, Saturday or Sunday (it varies), 2:30 p.m.

Lacroix-Saint-Ouen, irregularly held (call for dates and times).
Laon, Saturday, 2:30 p.m.
Le Puy, Thursday, Monday, and 15th day of month, 2 p.m.

Lyon, Monday and Wednesday, 2 p.m.

Mâcon, Saturday, 2:30 p.m.
Marseille, Wednesday, Friday, and Saturday,
  2:30 p.m.
Meaux, Saturday and Sunday, 2 p.m.
Montreuil-sur-Mer, Saturday and last
  Sunday of month, 3 p.m.

Nantes, Monday, Wednesday, and Friday, 2
  p.m.
Nogent-le-Rotrou, Saturday, 2 p.m.

Paris (Hôtel Drouot), daily, 2 p.m.
Pontoise, Monday and last Saturday of month,
  2:30 p.m.

Saint-Brieuc, Tuesday, 2 p.m.
Saint-Germain-en-Laye, Wednesday, 10 a.m.
  and 2 p.m.
Semur-en-Auxois, Sunday, 2 p.m.

Vannes (Hôtel des Ventes), Saturday, 2 p.m.
Verdun, Saturday, 2 p.m.
Vervins, Wednesday and Friday, 2:30 p.m.,
  Saturday, 10 a.m.
Vire (Hôtel des Ventes), Saturday, 2:30 p.m.
Vitry-le-François, first and third Monday, 2
  p.m.

# List of Illustrations

# List of Maps

# Maps of France

The map on this page is the key map to the detailed maps on the following pages.. Page numbers on this map refer to the following pages.

Each town location listed is mentioned in the text: only locations with at least one flea market, one antiques show or fair, or a public auction hall are listed.

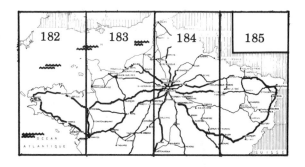

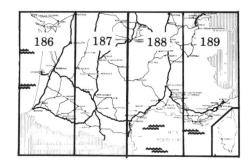

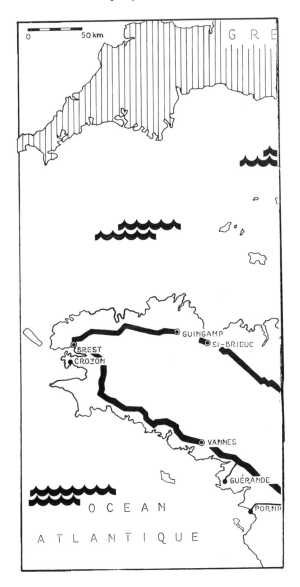

| | |
|---|---|
| ▰ Autoroute | ◉ City listed in text |
| — Main Road | • Town listed in text |

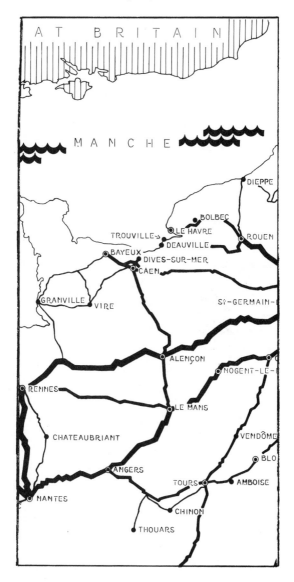

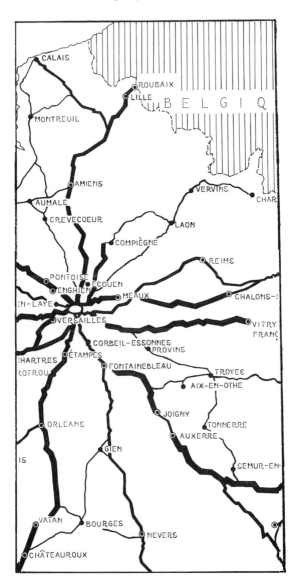

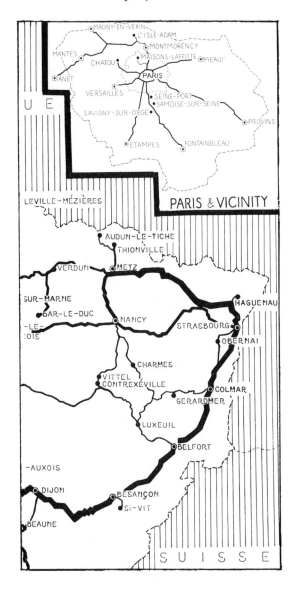

PARIS & VICINITY

MAGNY-EN-VEXIN
L'ISLE-ADAM
MONTMORENCY
MANTES
CHATOU
MAISONS-LAFFITTE
MEAUX
ANET
PARIS
VERSAILLES
SEINE-PORT
SAMOISE-SUR-SEINE
SAVIGNY-SUR-ORGE
PROVINS
ETAMPES
FONTAINBLEAU

LEVILLE-MÉZIÈRES

AUDUN-LE-TICHE
THIONVILLE
VERDUN
METZ
SUR-MARNE
BAR-LE-DUC
HAGUENAU
NANCY
STRASBOURG
-LE-
OIS
OBERNAI
CHARMES
VITTEL
CONTREXÉVILLE
COLMAR
GERARDMER
LUXEUIL
BELFORT
-AUXOIS
DIJON
BESANÇON
St-VIT
BEAUNE

S U I S S E

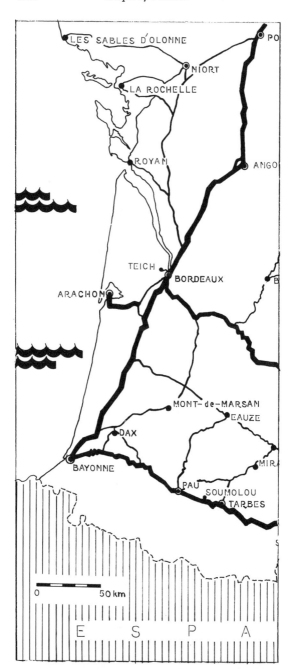

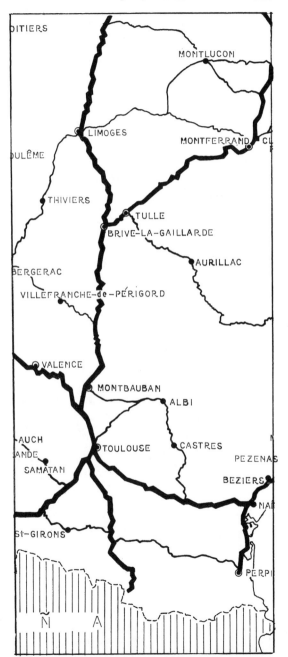

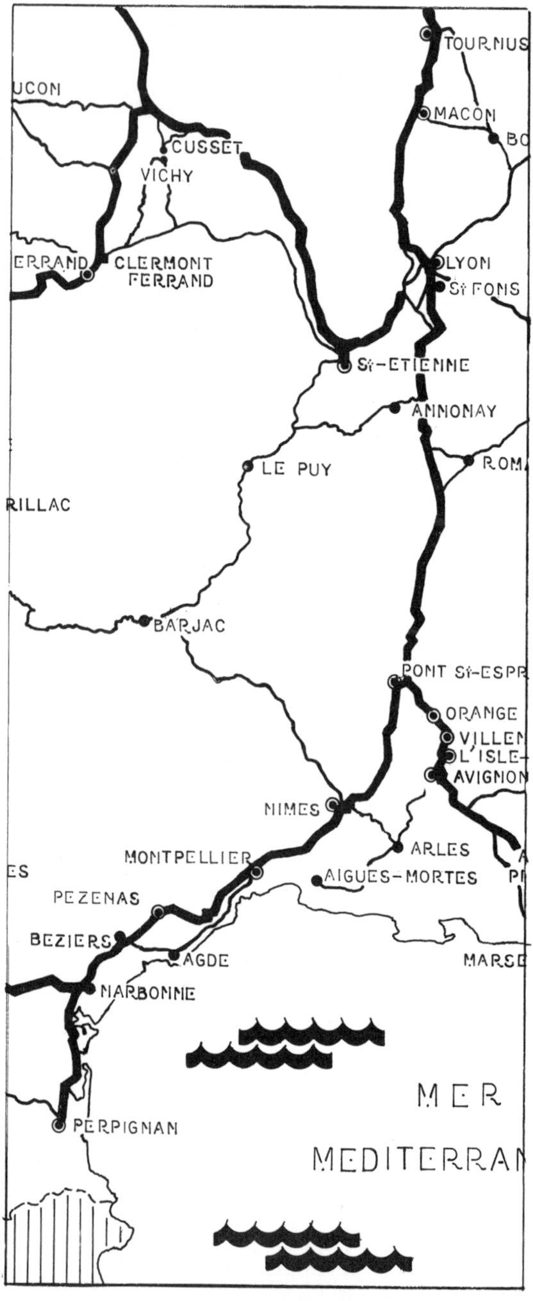

TOURNUS

MACON

BO

UCON

CUSSET

VICHY

ERRAND

CLERMONT
FERRAND

LYON

St FONS

St-ETIENNE

ANNONAY

LE PUY

ROM

RILLAC

BARJAC

PONT St-ESPR

ORANGE

VILLEN

L'ISLE-

AVIGNON

NIMES

MONTPELLIER

ARLES

A

PI

ES

AIGUES-MORTES

PEZENAS

BEZIERS

AGDE

MARSE

NARBONNE

PERPIGNAN

MER

MEDITERRAN

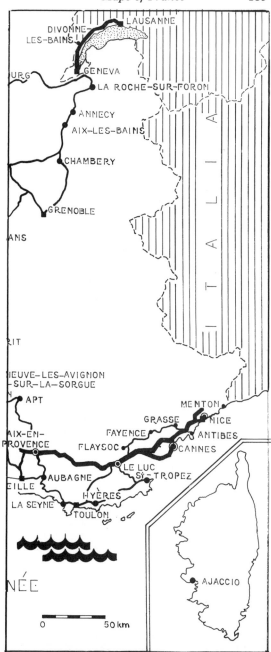

DIVONNE-
LES-BAINS
LAUSANNE
GENEVA
URG
LA ROCHE-SUR-FORON
ANNECY
AIX-LES-BAINS
CHAMBERY
GRENOBLE
ANS
RIT
ITALIA
NEUVE-LES-AVIGNON
-SUR-LA-SORGUE
APT
MENTON
GRASSE
NICE
FAYENCE
ANTIBES
AIX-EN-
PROVENCE
FLAYSOC
CANNES
LE LUC
St-TROPEZ
AUBAGNE
EILLE
HYÈRES
LA SEYNE
TOULON
NÉE
AJACCIO
0        50 km

# Index

# Will You Help?

Time Passes, events change. Almost as soon as this book went to the printer, things changed: some shows moved location, others were cancelled, others increased in size or scope, others gained a focus on a particular type of item. Some flea markets may move because of urban renewal or other reasons.

Won't you please let us know? If you do, we'll be able to improve future editions of this book. Then, future readers can benefit from your findings.

Either tear out this page, or feel free to use other sheets of paper.

Sincerely, Travel Keys.

What did you find different?

What problems did you find?

Are there any tricks you know to avoid this problem?

What markets or fairs moved time or place?

What was your greatest success and most wonderful find?

Thank you very much!

Please send your comments to:

Travel Keys
P.O. Box 160691
Sacramento, Calif. 95816 U.S.A.

# Will You Help?

Time Passes, events change. Almost as soon as this book went to the printer, things changed: some shows moved location, others were cancelled, others increased in size or scope, others gained a focus on a particular type of item. Some flea markets may move because of urban renewal or other reasons.

Won't you please let us know? If you do, we'll be able to improve future editions of this book. Then, future readers can benefit from your findings.

Either tear out this page, or feel free to use other sheets of paper.

Sincerely, Travel Keys.

What did you find different?

What problems did you find?

Are there any tricks you know to avoid this problem?

What markets or fairs moved time or place?

What was your greatest success and most wonderful find?

Thank you very much!

Please send your comments to:

Travel Keys
P.O. Box 160691
Sacramento, Calif. 95816 U.S.A.

# Order Blank

We'll ship your order postpaid as soon as we receive it and a check, money order, or credit card information.

*Title*                                          *Total*

Manston's Travel Key Guides

Manston's Flea Markets of Britain $9.95 _____

Manston's Flea Markets of France $9.95 _____

Manston's Flea Markets of Germany $9.95 _____

Manston's Travel Key Europe $9.95      _____

Collins Phrase Books

French Phrase Book $4.95                  _____

German Phrase Book $4.95                  _____

Greek Phrase Book $4.95                   _____

Italian Phrase Book $4.95                 _____

Spanish Phrase Book $4.95                 _____

Californians add sales tax:            _____
Postage & handling included            | 0 . 00 |
Overseas Airmail: Add $8.20 per        _____
book

**Total:**                      $       _____

*Payment by check:*
Please make checks and money orders payable to Travel Keys.

If your check is not drawn on a U.S. bank, please send in your currency and add equivalent of $4.00 to cover costs of exchange.

Please do not send checks drawn on a foreign bank in U.S. dollars.

*(Over, please for credit cards orders and mailing address for orders)*

*Credit card orders:*

We accept VISA and MasterCard, as well as Access and Carte Bleu. Credit card orders may be placed by telephone as well as by mail.

You may call (916) 452-5200 24 hours a day for credit card orders.

For all credit card orders, we need:

Credit Card number:

Expiration Date:

4-Digit Bank # (M/C only):

Signature:

Date:

*Send order to:*

Name:

Address:

City, State or Province:

Zip or postal code:

Your daytime telephone number:

# Notes

# Notes

# Notes

# Notes

# Notes

*About the Author:*

Peter B. Manston, travel and food writer, has been roaming through Europe for years, searching for antique fairs and street markets, collectors' meets and auctions for almost as long. He's collected centuries' old silver, glass, crystal, and wood carvings.

His fascination with antiques and collectables and the hunt for them are clearly evident in the details of the markets, fairs, and auctions described: not only how large each one is, but what types of items predominate, how to find them, and more.

He has organized the material to make it easy to use this book, and hopes you'll find as many delightful and valuable items as he has.

Good Luck and Happy Hunting!